Learning CFEngine 3

Diego Zamboni

Beijing · Cambridge · Farnham · Köln · Sebastopol · Tokyo

Learning CFEngine 3
by Diego Zamboni

Published by O'Reilly Media, Inc., 1005 Gravenstein Highway North, Sebastopol, CA 95472.

O'Reilly books may be purchased for educational, business, or sales promotional use. Online editions are also available for most titles (*http://my.safaribooksonline.com*). For more information, contact our corporate/institutional sales department: (800) 998-9938 or *corporate@oreilly.com*.

Editors: Andy Oram and Mike Hendrickson	**Cover Designer:** Karen Montgomery
Production Editor: Dan Fauxsmith	**Interior Designer:** David Futato
Proofreader: O'Reilly Production Services	**Illustrator:** Robert Romano

Revision History for the First Edition:
   2012-03-16   First release
See *http://oreilly.com/catalog/errata.csp?isbn=9781449312206* for release details.

ISBN: 978-1-449-31220-6

[LSI]

1331902715

Table of Contents

Foreword vii

Preface xi

1. Introduction 1
How to Achieve Automation   3
   Home-Grown Scripts   3
   Specialized Tools for Automation   4
Why CFEngine?   6
A Brief History of CFEngine   7
Versions of CFEngine   8

2. Getting Started with CFEngine 11
Installing CFEngine   11
   Installing the Community Edition from Source   12
   Installing the Community Edition from Binary Packages   15
   Installing the Commercial Edition   15
Finishing the Installation and Bootstrapping   16
Auxiliary Files   18
Your First CFEngine Policy   18

3. CFEngine Basics 23
Basic Principles   23
   Desired-State Configuration   23
   Basic CFEngine Operations   24
   Promise Theory   25
   Convergent Configuration   27
CFEngine Components   27
A First Example   30
CFEngine Policy Structure   32
   Data Types and Variables in CFEngine   33

Classes and Decision Making   37
Containers   41
Normal Ordering   51
Looping in CFEngine   53
Thinking in CFEngine   56
Clients and Servers   57
CFEngine Server Configuration   59
Updating Client Files from the Server   60
CFEngine Remote Execution Using cf-runagent   63
CFEngine Information Resources   65
Manuals and Official Guides   65
CFEngine Standard Library   66
CFEngine Solutions Guide   66
CFEngine Design Center   66
Community Forums   67
CFEngine Bug Tracker   67
Other Community Resources   67
Recommended Reading Order   67

4. Using CFEngine 69
Initial System Configuration   69
Editing /etc/sysctl.conf   69
Editing /etc/sshd_config   78
Editing /etc/inittab   83
Configuration Files with Variable Content   86
User Management   91
Software Installation   95
Package-Based Software Management   95
Manual Software Management   99
Using CFEngine for Security   107
Policy Enforcement   107
Security Scanning   113

5. CFEngine Tips, Tricks, and Patterns 119
Hierarchical Copying   119
Passing Name-Value Pairs to Bundles   126
Setting Default Values for Bundle Parameters   129
Using Classes as Configuration Mechanisms   130
Generic Tasks Using Lists and Array Indices   133
Defining Classes for Groups of Hosts   136
Controlling Promise Execution Order   138

6. Advanced Topics **141**

Setting Up Multiple CFEngine Environments   141

Using a Version-Control System to Separate Environments   145

Flow of Development and Deployment   146

CFEngine Testing   147

Behavioral Testing for CFEngine Policies   147

Unit Testing for CFEngine Policies   148

Where to from Here?   154

Appendix: Editing CFEngine 3 Configurations in Emacs **157**

Foreword

The history of "Unix" system configuration has been a fascinating ride that took us from shell scripting to sophisticated knowledge-oriented tools.

I still recall arriving in San Diego in 1997 for the USENIX/LISA conference, just three years after releasing CFEngine to the wider world as a GNU Free Software distribution. I walked through the door from conference registration and the first person I met looked at my badge and said: "Hey, you're Mark Burgess—you wrote CFEngine!" That was my first exposure to the power of community.

Free Open Source Software (FOSS) was a kind of Berlin Wall moment for the software industry, removing the barriers to contributing innovative ideas that had been closed off by fearful corporate protectionism. Perhaps ironically, "free software" was the door-opener to innovation that enabled Internet commerce to take off—transforming Richard Stallman's vision of "free speech" into a definite focus on "free beer," but with the importance of community social networks strongly emphasized.

To me, what was important about FOSS was that it enabled research and development to flourish and find a willing audience, all without anyone's approval. For CFEngine, this was central to overcoming limitations steeped in the past.

When I began writing CFEngine in 1993, inspired by colleagues at Oslo University, the main problem lay in handling a diversity of operating systems. There were many more flavors of Unix-like OS back then, and they were much more different than they are today. Writing any kind of script was a nightmare of exception logic: "If this is SunOS 4.x or Ultrix, but not SunOS 4.1 or anything at the Chemistry department, and by the way patch 1234 is not installed, then..."

Such scripts appealed to a generation of "Large Installation System Administrators," who had deep system experience and basic programming skills. Alas, in such a script, you couldn't see the intention for the logic, so many scripts were thrown away and rewritten in the latest cool scripting language each time someone arrived or left. It was a time-wasting chaos.

The separation of "intended outcome" from the detailed imperative coding was the first purpose of a specialized language for system administration, i.e., making infrastructure documentation of intent rather than unreadable code—or as declarative programmers would say, the separation of "what" from "how."

As a theoretical physicist, in postdoctoral purgatory, instinct moved me to look into the scientific literature of the subject of system management, and I discovered that there was very little work done in the field of host configuration. As I left the conference in 1997, I got sick on the plane, and this gave me an idea. A year later, I went back to the LISA conference and wrote down a research manifesto for "autonomic self-healing systems" called Computer Immunology. IBM's autononomic computing initiative followed a few years later. Those were heady days of CFEngine history, filled with excitement and discovery of principles like "convergence" and "adaptive locking." At LISA 98, I presented "Computer Immunology" in one hall of the conference while Tom Perrine (then of the San Diego Supercomputing Center, later LOPSA president) opened his talk in the next room with the flattering words: "I owe Mark Burgess more beer than I can afford..." And thus the partnership between science and community was begun.

CFEngines 1 and 2 took the world by storm. No one really knows how many agents are running out there, but it runs into the many millions. A large covert community still thrives behind the scenes, making little noise. Recently, a large internet retailer indicated a million computers running CFEngine 2, saying: "Well, it just works." Similar stories abound.

Even so, CFEngine had rough edges, and we saw plenty of room for improvement. As the Web 2.0 companies were emerging in the 2000s, other tools began to emerge for configuration, bringing back the idea of "Script It Yourself" to engage a generation of web programmers impatient with the idea of system administration getting in the way of more agile methods. Software packaging developed into an important simplification of the configuration—but much too simplistic to support the required competitive differentiation in an application-driven era of IT. From this tension, the idea of DevOps began to emerge and configuration moved back in the direction of custom coding, aided by "easy language frameworks" like Ruby.

By this time, I had developed a new model for CFEngine that captured its famous distributed autonomy, and had brought CFEngine its documentable scalability and security properties. This model came to be known as Promise Theory, and as I developed and tested the idea from 2004-2007 I realized that the challenge was not at all about scripting or programming, but really about knowledge and documentation ("The Third Wave of IT"). The CFEngine answer was thus to pursue the original idea: that understanding infrastructure is about modelling intent, not about one-size-fits-all commodity packaging. CFEngine 3 should not be code development, but declaration of intent (promises).

In early 2008, almost ten years after the Computer Immunology manifesto, I began coding CFEngine 3—a strict implementation of my understanding of the best that science and community experience had uncovered—to promote a technology direction that could go beyond the immediate needs to datacentres and create a legacy for dealing with scale, complexity, and agility for the coming decade.

And today? In today's environment where everything seems steeped in web programming, source code seems ironically less important than during the formative rebellion of FOSS; Application Program Interfaces (APIs) are the "new open source," but the danger lies in being pulled back into opaque custom scripting, that conflates "what" with "how."

Today, there is a CFEngine company as well as a vibrant community that supports and develops future innovation in the CFEngine technology; and users are moving to the next level: Knowledge Driven Configuration Management.

Today, I am also proud and a little humbled to read Diego's fine book about this new challenge, and finally join the ranks of the O'Reilly bestiary. He has been able to present CFEngine in a way that I was never able to do, and make it accessible to readers of all levels and backgrounds. As one community member wrote, this is the tutorial the CFEngine never had.

The future of system administration is once again in the making, with recyclable resource management now reaching the platform level through Cloud thinking, applications growing from complex integrations of FOSS sub-systems, and datacenters flaring like novae around us. In these heavens, CFEngine is still a guiding star, paving the way towards a new generation of knowledge-based infrastructure engineering.

—Mark Burgess
Founder and CTO of CFEngine
Oslo, February 2012

Preface

This is a book about system administration. As any system administrator knows, there is no professional joy greater than seeing systems work consistently and perform their tasks flawlessly. And the joy is even greater if the systems need as little human attention as possible. Automating system administration tasks is not only a source of pride, but also an urgent need once the number of machines under our control grows beyond a very small number, as it is otherwise impossible to keep track of everything by hand. The number and complexity of computer systems have grown exponentially over the years, to the point where managing them by hand has become impossible for any single person. To this effect, CFEngine can help. CFEngine is a useful automation tool, but it goes well beyond that. It provides you with a framework to manage and implement IT infrastructure in a sustainable, scalable, and efficient manner. It allows you to elevate your thinking about systems so that you can focus on the higher-level issues of design, implementation, and maintenance, while having the certainty that lower-level details are handled for you automatically.

My road to writing this book started over 20 years ago, when I first became a Unix sysadmin at my university, working back then on a DECstation 5000 running Ultrix, a few SGI machines with Irix, and a Cray Y-MP/400 supercomputer with UNICOS. Even in that relatively simple environment, the challenges of doing everything by hand quickly became apparent. Over the years I have appreciated more and more the advantages of automating as much as possible all system management tasks. I first heard of CFEngine (still in version 1 back then) during my early years as a sysadmin, and over the years I loosely followed its development. Then in 2009 I got to work with CFEngine 3, and was immediately impressed with its flexibility and power. I also realized that a book about it was needed to help beginners overcome many of the questions that surface while learning to use it. Much of the literature at the time was focused on CFEngine 2, and CFEngine 3 is a completely new version, with vast improvements in all its aspects, including a completely new syntax.

It is a pleasure to finally deliver this book to you, and I hope you enjoy it.

Who Is This Book For?

This book is for you if you are a system administrator who is interested in learning new tools and techniques for making your life easier. I assume throughout the book that you are relatively well versed in system administration techniques, mostly about Unix-style operating systems. It will also help in some parts if you are familiar with regular expressions. I do not assume you know anything about CFEngine, but if you already know it, I am sure you will still find some interesting tidbits and learn some new techniques.

This book is not a complete reference to CFEngine. It is a "learning" book. The CFEngine manuals are an excellent source of reference information, and the text contains numerous references (mostly in the form of links embedded in the electronic versions of this book) to the appropriate documentation.

Overview of the Book

This book is organized as a progressive tutorial and is meant to be read from start to finish. If you already know some of the concepts you may be able to skip some of the basic sections. However, keep in mind that there are many examples and concepts that are developed over the course of a whole chapter (this is particularly true for Chapter 4), so you may be missing some of the context if you skip ahead.

On the other hand, I have read enough books myself to know that most people are unlikely to read it from start to finish. So most sections are as self-contained as possible without being repetitive, and with ample references to other sections when necessary. This book consists of six chapters:

Chapter 1 is for motivation and historical perspective. It describes the many benefits that can be obtained through pervasive system automation, and describes the history and versions of CFEngine.

Chapter 2 is for quick and easy practice. In it I will walk you through getting CFEngine up and running on your system, and then writing and executing your first CFEngine policy.

Chapter 3 gives you a needed conceptual foundation. In it you will still see plenty of examples and CFEngine code, but with an eye on teaching you the basic principles of how CFEngine works, both from a theoretical (e.g., promise theory) and practical (e.g., language structure and features) point of view. You will also find pointers to many useful sources of information about CFEngine. You will probably refer back to this chapter often as you read through the rest of the book.

Chapter 4 is for really diving in. In it we will go through many examples of different tasks you can perform using CFEngine, explaining each one of them in detail. Through this chapter you will see many examples that you can (hopefully) use as-they-are for performing some real tasks, but you will also learn the underlying concepts that will be useful for adapting those examples, and for coming up with your own CFEngine policies.

Chapter 5 summarizes some generic tricks and patterns that you can use in CFEngine to achieve certain results. These are not specific recipes, but rather more generic techniques that you should learn to adapt and use in your own policies.

Finally, in Chapter 6 we will explore two topics that you may not need right away, but that will make your life easier in the future: maintaining separate CFEngine environments (for example, for development, testing and production) and testing mechanisms for CFEngine.

In the Appendix, contributed by Ted Zlatanov, you will find a detailed explanation of how to use Emacs to edit CFEngine policy files. Ted is the author and maintainer of cfengine-mode for Emacs.

As you read through the book, I encourage you to try out the examples. Preferably type them in yourself! I have learned from experience that typing the code (rather than downloading or copy/pasting it) helps tremendously to better understand a new language. It lets you develop a feeling for the code, it lets you make mistakes and figure out how to fix them, and it makes it easier to experiment and modify the examples. If you definitely don't have the time or inclination to type them, you can download all the examples in this book from *http://cf-learn.info/code.html*, either individually or as a whole.

Online Resources

You can find the web page for this book at *http://cf-learn.info/*. In it you can find code samples, errata, a discussion forum, a CFEngine-related blog and many other resources that you may find useful. I encourage you to visit, and of course to participate in the forum with suggestions, comments, or any other feedback.

If you are reading an electronic version of this book, you will find that most CFEngine keywords in the text, and some other concepts, are links that will take you to the corresponding part of the CFEngine Reference Manual.

You can find me on Twitter at *http://twitter.com/zzamboni*.

You will find references to many other CFEngine-related resources in "CFEngine Information Resources" on page 65.

Conventions Used in This Book

The following typographical conventions are used in this book:

Italic
> Indicates new terms, URLs, email addresses, filenames, and file extensions.

`Constant width`
> Used for program listings, as well as within paragraphs to refer to program elements such as variable or function names, CFEngine bundle and body names, databases, data types, environment variables, statements, and keywords.

`Constant width bold`
> Shows commands or other text that should be typed literally by the user.

`Constant width italic`
> Shows text that should be replaced with user-supplied values or by values determined by context.

 This icon signifies a tip, suggestion, or general note.

 This icon indicates a warning or caution.

Using Code Examples

This book is here to help you get your job done. In general, you may use the code in this book in your programs and documentation. You do not need to contact us for permission unless you're reproducing a significant portion of the code. For example, writing a program that uses several chunks of code from this book does not require permission. Selling or distributing a CD-ROM of examples from O'Reilly books does require permission. Answering a question by citing this book and quoting example code does not require permission. Incorporating a significant amount of example code from this book into your product's documentation does require permission.

We appreciate, but do not require, attribution. An attribution usually includes the title, author, publisher, and ISBN. For example: "*Learning CFEngine 3* by Diego Zamboni (O'Reilly). Copyright 2012 Diego Zamboni, 9781449312206."

If you feel your use of code examples falls outside fair use or the permission given above, feel free to contact us at *permissions@oreilly.com*.

Safari® Books Online

 Safari Books Online (*www.safaribooksonline.com*) is an on-demand digital library that delivers expert content in both book and video form from the world's leading authors in technology and business.

Technology professionals, software developers, web designers, and business and creative professionals use Safari Books Online as their primary resource for research, problem solving, learning, and certification training.

Safari Books Online offers a range of product mixes and pricing programs for organizations, government agencies, and individuals. Subscribers have access to thousands of books, training videos, and prepublication manuscripts in one fully searchable database from publishers like O'Reilly Media, Prentice Hall Professional, Addison-Wesley Professional, Microsoft Press, Sams, Que, Peachpit Press, Focal Press, Cisco Press, John Wiley & Sons, Syngress, Morgan Kaufmann, IBM Redbooks, Packt, Adobe Press, FT Press, Apress, Manning, New Riders, McGraw-Hill, Jones & Bartlett, Course Technology, and dozens more. For more information about Safari Books Online, please visit us online.

How to Contact Us

Please address comments and questions concerning this book to the publisher:

> O'Reilly Media, Inc.
> 1005 Gravenstein Highway North
> Sebastopol, CA 95472
> 800-998-9938 (in the United States or Canada)
> 707-829-0515 (international or local)
> 707-829-0104 (fax)

We have a web page for this book, where we list errata, examples, and any additional information. You can access this page at:

> *http://www.oreilly.com/catalog/9781449312206/*

You can also find many resources, including all the code samples, at the author's web page for the book, which you can access at:

> *http://cf-learn.info/*

To comment or ask technical questions about this book, visit the discussion forum at *http://cf-learn.info/discussion.html*, or send email to:

> *bookquestions@oreilly.com*

For more information about our books, courses, conferences, and news, see our website at *http://www.oreilly.com*.

Find us on Facebook: *http://facebook.com/oreilly*

Follow us on Twitter: *http://twitter.com/oreillymedia*

Watch us on YouTube: *http://www.youtube.com/oreillymedia*

Acknowledgments

There were a lot of people who helped in the making of this book. I would like to thank my editor at O'Reilly Media, Andy Oram, who guided me and helped me through the process. After working with him, I know why O'Reilly books are so good. Beyond simply providing editorial advice, he immersed himself in the topic, researched and learned it, asked me hard questions, and pointed me to interesting resources. His friendly but firm guidance kept me going and made it possible for me finish this book.

I would like to thank my technical reviewers, Mark Burgess and Jesse Becker, for their insightful and useful feedback. Their comments ranged from details about wording or the indentation of the examples, to high-level conceptual observations that made me rethink the focus of entire sections of the book. Their commentary made this book vastly better than it was before. Mark is also the original author of CFEngine, so without him and his work this book would not exist at all.

Halfway through writing this book (and partly as a result of it) I started a new job at CFEngine AS, the company behind CFEngine. I could not have found a better work environment, nor a more motivated and talented group of colleagues. They provided encouragement, feedback and useful discussions. Thank you Sue Paludo, Joe Netzel, Matt Richards, Eystein Stenberg, Mark Burgess, Christian Figenschou, Thomas Ryd, Volker Hilsheimer, Geir Nygård, Jon Henrik Bjørnstad, Mikhail Gusarov, Sigurd Teigen, Nakarin Phooripoom, Bishwa Shrestha, Dan Klein, Dmitry Shevchenko, Maciej Mrowiec, Maciej Patucha, Nishes Joshi, Sudhir Pandey, Nili Gafni, Steve Curry, Steve Clarence, Mark deVisser, Marty Udisches, Tom Buck, Knut Stålen, Jon Rioja, Elena Culai, Beth Kaiser, Kristin Tobiassen, Sam Najork, and Carol Dolge.

CFEngine has an amazing and active user community, and working with such a community has always been a pleasure and an incredible learning experience. I would like to thank Aleksey Tsalolikhin (who kindly gave me permission to use his WordPress-installation policy in Chapter 4), Ted Zlatanov (who maintains the excellent cfengine-mode for Emacs, and who contributed the Appendix), Neil Watson (whose writing and posts have taught me so much about CFEngine), Mike Svoboda (who has never hesitated to share complex real-world CFEngine policies for everyone to use), Jesse Becker (who started *http://cfengineers.org/*, and gave me excellent feedback about the drafts of this book), Ben Bomgardner, Marco Marongiu, Nick Anderson, Seva Gluschenko, Nicolas Charles, Jonathan Clarke, and many others too numerous to mention.

I would like to offer a special mention to the staff at O'Reilly Media, who made my life as an author much easier by always providing friendly and competent support and information. In particular I need to mention Sanders Kleinfeld, who expertly helped me understand and set up the syntax highlighting used in the electronic versions of this book (and which I think greatly enhances the readability of examples).

This book started life during November 2010 in the "Pragmatic Programmers Writing Month" or PragProWriMo. This is an event designed to mimic the well known "NaNo-WriMo", but for technical books. For one month, I committed to writing two pages every day, and from this effort the very first draft of this book was born. During this process I had the support and encouragement of a wonderful group of people, including Susannah Pfalzer, Michael Swaine, Travis Swicegood, Raymond Yee and Bob Cochran. I also used *http://750words.com/*, a wonderful tool for writers created by Buster Benson and which helped me stay motivated throughout the month.

And of course, my life and work would not be the same without my family. My wife Susana has provided me with love, inspiration and encouragement, not to mention that, being also a sysadmin, she gave me some expert feedback on the book from the point of view of its target audience. And our two beautiful daughters Karina and Fabiola have, as always, been the joy of my life and a constant source of amazement and happiness. They all endured me spending many nights, weekends and off-hours working on "the book," while keeping me sane with their love and support. *Gracias mis bellas.*

## CHAPTER 1

Introduction

Every time someone logs onto a system by hand, they
jeopardize everyone's understanding of the system.

—Mark Burgess, author of CFEngine

If you are a computer user of any type, you rely on automation every day. Their ability to automate things is what makes computers useful, after all. Nobody adds up the columns in a spreadsheet by hand; we all let a formula do it for us. And instead of getting up in the middle of the night to rotate log files, a system administrator sets an automated job to do it. In fact, if you are a system administrator, you should rely much more on automation than any other type of computer user. If you take care of only a few machines, doing things by hand is perhaps not so bad—you can easily perform most necessary tasks by hand. But as the number of machines under your control grows, keeping them in working order, in a consistent state, and in a desired state (according to whatever needs they serve) can be a daunting task.

We live in an age of apparently infinitely-growing data centers. Think of Google, Facebook, or any other large Internet service. They can scale to serve hundreds of millions of users because they have enormous data centers performing all those operations, with hundreds of thousands of machines (perhaps even millions) at their disposal. Do you think an army of sysadmins is running around those data centers, fixing things, logging into machines to execute commands? Of course not (well, in some cases they might, but they really should not be doing that!). This would be a completely untenable and unscalable proposition. What these big companies do is automate the hell out of everything they need to do. In this way, they can be assured that their servers will be in an uniform and predictable state *automatically*. They can save their human system administrators for dealing with unexpected problems that the machines cannot solve on their own.

You should do this too.

The Third Wave of IT Engineering

Alvin Toffler in his books *Future Shock* and *The Third Wave* describes three waves of human society: the first wave was the agricultural society—tending the land with animal-assisted strength, each person, home, or family mostly self-sufficient. The second wave is the industrial age—mastering the environment through machine-assisted strength, large production chains, big corporations, big machines, and extreme specialization of labor, which leads to a fundamental divide between the rich factory owners and the poor workers. The third wave is the knowledge age, in which information and knowledge are the most valuable assets, characterized by the existence and wide availability of advanced technologies ("machine-assisted brain"), and which allows for personalization of products and services to a degree never before available. Since the second half of the 20th century, most human societies have been moving towards the Third Wave.

These same waves can be identified in systems management. The first wave consisted of individual system administrations tending to small-to-medium organizations, with ad-hoc (and often manual) methods. The large IT organizations and corporations, with their production-line mentality toward system administration, are the second wave, and led to extreme specialization of knowledge and cookie-cutter systems (think of "Gold Images") that are extremely difficult to customize and modify. The third wave of systems management is the age of personalization and flexibility. Nowadays anyone can be a sysadmin, and everyone can have technology and services customized to their own needs and preferences. This requires extreme agility in systems management, which can only be achieved through automation.

DevOps and Automation

In recent years, the DevOps movement has appeared and has grown in popularity and importance, in response to the need to speed up the development-deployment cycle. The term is a contraction of "Development" and "Operations," and corresponds to the general idea of achieving better collaboration and integration between development and IT operations. Traditionally, these two tasks have been performed by completely separate groups of people. However, the Third Wave requirements of agility, configurability, and flexibility mean that a much tighter integration is needed. DevOps, among other principles, encourages developers to be in charge of deploying their own applications, thus short-cutting the deployment cycle. In some organizations, developers may deploy their code many times during a day. System automation plays a crucial role in enabling DevOps, by hiding much of the complexity of operations tasks.

Furthermore, automation elevates our way of thinking about systems. Once a task is automated, it becomes possible to think about the higher-level issues surrounding our systems, and to think more about *what* than *how*. For example, without automation, we have to think about how and when to rotate the log files on Solaris, how to do it on different Linux distributions, how to do it on Windows, and so on. Once these low-level tasks are automated, we can simply say "rotate the log files on all systems". And once this is done, we can go to an even higher level, and group log rotation with other tasks and just say "do system maintenance," with the knowledge that all the low-level tasks that compose this goal will be done predictably and efficiently.

But you are only in charge of 100 machines, perhaps? 15? 5? Only one, your own workstation? The basic premise holds. If you are doing things by hand, you are taking longer to do things than it should, you risk making mistakes, and you are unnecessarily repeating tasks that should be automated. Humans are good at thinking; computers are good at repetition. What this means is that you should design the solution, and then let the machine execute it. Of course, you should do the necessary tasks by hand once or maybe twice, to figure out exactly what needs to be done. After all, a computer will not be able to figure out by itself (in most cases) the exact disk partitioning scheme that needs to be used in your database servers, or select the parameters that need to go into your *sshd* configuration file, or write the script that needs to run to back up your workstation into your external USB disk every time you plug it in. But once you've got those steps figured out, there is no reason to continue doing them by hand. The machine can repeat those steps exactly right, in the correct order, and at the correct moment every single time, regardless of the time of day or whether you are sick or on vacation.

How to Achieve Automation

There are different ways to automate system administration. You already know which one I am going to advocate, but for the sake of completeness I will discuss a few of them.

Home-Grown Scripts

The first step, and a necessary one for sysadmins to understand the work involved in automating a system, is to write home-grown scripts. Once you figure out the steps needed to partition that disk, you put them in a shell script so that you don't forget. Maybe you write the description in a wiki or your blog. The trick is to document the steps somewhere so that you can recall them. Once you figure out the precise installation options to boot from the SAN, you write them down in your notebook, and if you are really disciplined you create a custom Anaconda configuration file to be able to repeat them. Once you figure out the *rsync* options for backing up your machine, you write a shell script to run it. Once you decide on the appropriate *sshd* options, you write a *perl* or *sed* script to insert them into the */etc/ssh/sshd_config* file.

But you still have to remember to run the backup script by hand every time you plug in your external disk. Or someday you figure out installation options that work better, but commit them to memory instead of updating your notebook or your Anaconda script. Or your needs change and you update your personal copy of the partitioning shell script, but fail to update your wiki or blog or document.

Then one day you are home sick, and no one else knows which script to run, or how to run it. Or they find your documentation and follow it, but it's outdated and it doesn't work, or even worse: it works but produces results that will cause problems later on, and will be very hard to track to this particular point in time. Or you forget and run your *sshd*-configuration script twice on the same machine, and unless you have been very careful in developing it, the configuration file is ruined because the script didn't find its expected input. Did the script make a backup of the original file before modifying it? Oops.

The thing is, when you use ad-hoc tools for automation, you are still doing a large part of the process by hand, you are still relying on your discipline to keep documentation updated, and you still have to remember to do the right things in the right order and at the right time. In other words, you are still mixing *what* to do with *how* to achieve it.

One day you are banging your head against the wall because you can't figure out how your colleague who is hiking in the Alps does the cleanup of temporary files in your database server, and you know he has a script but you don't know where to find it or how to run it. Or even if things go well, after using your home-grown tools for a while, you will find that complexity creeps into them from ever-changing requirements and necessary flexibility, and they become harder and harder to maintain. You start thinking there must be a better way to do it.

Specialized Tools for Automation

Over the years, a number of specialized tools have emerged for automating system configuration. Depending on the vendor, they may be called configuration management tools, provisioning tools, datacenter management tools, or a number of different terms. Strictly speaking, there are subtle differences in what the terms mean:

- *Configuration management* refers specifically to the handling of system information, including its hardware information, system configuration, and also things like physical location, owner, etc. CM tools often deal as well with the processes of defining, setting, storing, and modifying configurations, also possibly tied to standards such as ITIL (the Information Technology Infrastructure Library).

- *Provisioning* refers much more specifically to the act of preparing and configuring computing resources as needed. Provisioning management tools can usually deal with the processes needed to get physical machines installed and ready to use, generate configuration information, produce purchase orders, track the purchase and delivery process, and coordinate the necessary steps for physical and logical installation of new systems. In recent years, provisioning is often considered (and made easier) in the context of virtual machines, in which new systems can be created on demand with the desired configuration.

- *Datacenter management* often refers to the higher-level functions of running a large set of machines, from the logistics of physical arrangement to details such as keeping track of the amount of electricity and cooling needed, personnel schedules for 24-hour assistance, and so on.

In practice, certain aspects of these tools blend together. Most of them, at some point, need information about how the systems should be configured, and, through their own mechanisms, aid in getting the systems into that state.

There are a few products from big companies in this area. Two that you are certain to find in any discussion are IBM's Tivoli Provisioning Manager (TPM) and HP's Server and Network Automation suites. Both of these tools take the high-end approach: they require lots of resources, often several machines and large amounts of maintenance and configuration to install and operate. In exchange, they provide point-and-click operation, the ability to manage machines from their bare-metal installation through their entire lifecycle, even through decommissioning. Ultimately, the biggest advantage of these tools is that they come with the support of big companies, and they integrate well with other tools provided by the same companies for IT infrastructure management. Of course, the price tag for the tools and their support matches their complexity and size—they are targeted at big companies with big budgets.

In recent years, there has been a resurgence of interest in configuration management because systems and networks are growing in complexity, and people realize that manual management is simply not feasible. There are three big contenders from the open-source world: CFEngine, Chef, and Puppet (all of which, by now, also have commercial offerings).

CFEngine is the most mature of configuration management systems. It was first released in 1993, and is the oldest actively-maintained configuration management system. It has served as a reference point and inspiration for many of the newer tools, of which the two prime examples are Chef and Puppet. Its latest release, CFEngine 3, has many features that allow simple management of both small and large systems, providing extreme flexibility and agility in their management.

Puppet was inspired by CFEngine 2, and has a large and active community. It uses a specialized language to describe the desired state of the system. Chef in turn was inspired by Puppet, and was originally meant to address the ability to deploy systems "in the cloud," although it has since grown into a general and powerful systems-management tool. Both Chef and Puppet are written in Ruby.

CFEngine remains the most mature, actively-maintained, and one of the most widely-used configuration management tools. It has evolved over the years to address real needs in real systems, and is by now fine-tuned to the features and design that make it possible to automate very large numbers of systems in a scalable and manageable way.

Why CFEngine?

CFEngine can be used to automate any kind of computing infrastructure. For example, let us consider servers. Servers need consistent, repeatable, and observable configurations for many reasons: to bring them up quickly and reliably, to provide an environment where programs are known to run correctly, to track down problems by comparing the state to a known baseline, to ensure security on each system, and so on. But every time someone modifies a machine configuration by hand, the predictability of its state diminishes, due to manually-introduced errors or variations. Over time, for a large number of machines, their configuration will tend to differ enough to make managing them consistently extremely hard.

In server machines, CFEngine can be used for many different tasks, including (but not limited to) the following:

Configuration
> The configuration of both the base operating system and installed software can be easily handled using CFEngine, keeping them current and consistent.

User management
> CFEngine allows you to control user accounts and their characteristics. CFEngine gives you the high-level ability to indicate which user accounts are needed, and also the low-level power to control specific parameters such as passwords, expiration dates, etc.

Software installation
> Both off-the-shelf and custom software can be managed (including installation, upgrades, and removals) using CFEngine. CFEngine is designed to interact with the system's native package-management tools so that software is managed in an appropriate manner. CFEngine can also be used to manually install or remove software for which packages do not exist.

Looking at this list, you may wonder what is really the advantage of CFEngine, given that specialized tools exist already for all of these tasks. CFEngine provides the following advantages:

Flexibility
> CFEngine can help you easily maintain several types of machine configurations. In many cases, different types of servers are needed: web servers, database servers, authentication servers, print servers, and so on. With CFEngine, you need to define the configuration of each server type only once. Afterward, configuring a new machine is as easy as telling CFEngine the type of configuration to use.

Reusability
> CFEngine allows you to abstract common configuration tasks and conditions and reuse them in as many places as needed. As an example, you can define library components that perform common tasks such as software installation, user man-

agement, or text-file processing, and combine them to produce the exact configuration you need.

Multiple abstraction levels

CFEngine allows you to express very complex configurations at a very high level, hiding the implementation details unless you want to look at them. In this way, CFEngine allows you to express system configurations in human-readable form, which makes it easier to examine them for compliance, or to make high-level changes with minimum effort. However, the lower-level implementation details are accessible when you need to change them or examine how things are actually being implemented. This allows you to make the high-level policy specification independent of operating system details, with the system-specific implementation details hidden in the lower-level components.

Customization

CFEngine's ability to define different types of systems does not mean that all your systems have to be configured according to one of those predefined types. Quite the contrary! CFEngine makes it possible to specify each machine configuration in as much detail as needed. For a standard machine that only needs to adhere to the base defaults or one of your predefined machine types, you can simply specify it. But if you need a machine with a specialized configuration, one that is not repeated anywhere else in your network, or one which belongs to multiple classes (e.g., a backup web server that also doubles as a DNS server), CFEngine gives you the capability to express those needs in the policy without having to make ad-hoc, custom changes by hand anywhere.

Of course, these advantages are relevant for any piece of computing infrastructure. CFEngine is most commonly used to automate servers, but it can just as well be used to automate and control desktop machines, networking equipment (routers, switches, etc.), or other specialized appliances (VMware ESX servers, IDS appliances, etc.). CFEngine can be installed in many Linux-based appliances, but it can also be used to monitor and control those appliances remotely, if they have some form of remote-control interface.

A Brief History of CFEngine

CFEngine was created in 1993 by Mark Burgess at Oslo University in Norway to automate the configuration of Unix systems. CFEngine 1 was essentially a specialized language that allowed implicit if-then tests based on "classes" to determine what command should be executed on which systems, and which had a fixed set of actions that could be performed on each system (such as configuring */etc/resolv.conf*, mounting filesystems, and cleaning up temporary files).

CFEngine gained popularity, and in 2002 CFEngine 2 was released. This version of CFEngine was based already on research done by Burgess on the topics of computer immunology and convergent configuration. These put forward the idea that a configuration management system should bring a system towards its desired state gradually, fixing only what is necessary to bring it to its desired state. This characteristic greatly simplifies the deployment and implementation of a configuration management system. With home-grown scripts or any other tool that simply executes a sequence of steps, you have to be careful because running the same commands twice may break the system. The idea of convergent configuration means that actions should be taken only in the measure needed to bring the system to its desired state, and to make no unnecessary or additional changes once in that state.

As CFEngine's popularity grew, its language grew with it, and statements and features were added based on experience and identified needs. Author Mark Burgess embarked on a redesign phase, and the result was CFEngine 3, released in 2009. The new release was now supported by *promise theory*, developed by the author over the years of observing how CFEngine works and how it can bring a system to a predictable desired state by following a set of consistent principles. The syntax of the language was completely revamped to make it consistent and in line with promise theory. Under the new model, every CFEngine statement is a promise made by an object and with certain properties. This makes the language extremely simple, consistent, and extensible. Also new in CFEngine 3 was the idea of Knowledge Management. This means that a CFEngine policy can now also include high-level knowledge about the policy, including its intentions, and the language can be fully annotated to make it easier for people to understand the purpose of the policy and how it achieves its goals.

CFEngine 3 represents a big change from previous versions, particularly because it created an incompatible policy syntax. However, great benefits spring from the redesign of the language and the theory behind it. If necessary, the language can be expanded to include new promise types without modifying its basic structure.

Finally, CFEngine 3 was accompanied by the birth of a company (CFEngine AS) to provide commercial support and to produce commercial editions of CFEngine. Although the core of CFEngine is still (and will remain) open source, commercial versions include "enterprise" features that make it easier to install, configure, and administer machines in very large environments, including tight integration of reporting capabilities, simpler deployment mechanisms, integration with directory servers (LDAP), database support, and a graphical administration console.

Versions of CFEngine

CFEngine was born as an open-source project, and that has been one of its biggest strengths, since (like many open-source projects) it has created an active community of users who can look at the code to understand what is happening and how things work, who can submit bug fixes and patches, and who have kept CFEngine developers busy with feature requests and ideas. The main CFEngine version, now called "Community Edition," is still open source and available for free, and it includes the vast majority of the features of the language.

With the introduction of CFEngine 3 and the founding of CFEngine AS has come the introduction of a commercial version of CFEngine, called CFEngine Nova. It includes pre-built binary versions for many operating systems, including native Windows support (the Community edition can be compiled under Windows using Cygwin, but does not support many Windows-specific system features), and it also includes many convenience features, such as native support for database and LDAP connections, Windows registry examination and editing, support for creation and configuration of virtual machines, better reporting facilities, and full integration of knowledge management tools, including graphical tools to view policies and the knowledge generated from them.

In general terms, there are few things that Nova can do that the Community edition cannot. With enough tuning, you can achieve most basic tasks using the free version. What Nova gives you is a commercially-supported version (this is important in many companies), extended reporting features, advanced knowledge-management features, and the ability to do natively many tasks that would require external tools if you were using the Community edition (e.g., database connections and Windows registry operations). Nova also has an architecture designed to scale with all its features (such as reporting) to very large networks, while maintaining responsiveness.

In this book I will cover both Community and Nova, although I will try to stay away from Nova-specific features unless strictly needed, or unless we are explicitly discussing them. Nova-specific features will be clearly identified, so that you know not to expect them to work if you are using Community.

CFEngine Nova is a strict superset of Community in terms of the policy language, so it is easy to get started using Community, and when your needs grow or you need to ensure commercial support for your installation, you can easily upgrade to Nova and have your existing policies function flawlessly. Also of note is that all Nova-specific features of the CFEngine language are recognized as valid by CFEngine Community, but they are just non-functional. This means that you can write policy files with Nova features and run them on Community. They may not be functional, but they will not cause a crash or an error.

One difference of using Nova is, of course, that you do not get the source code for it. If you are not using one of the supported systems, you may be out of luck using it (admittedly, the list of supported systems is fairly large and includes most common Unix and Linux distributions, plus Windows). With Community, if you can get it to compile you can use it, and the requirements are fairly simple to provide, so there are good chances you will be able to compile it.

In the end, the choice between Community and Nova is up to you and your particular situation regarding needs, time, and budget. Both include the same basic technology and use exactly the same concepts for configuration management, so in any case you can rest assured that you are getting some of the most advanced and proven configuration-management technology available.

## CHAPTER 2

Getting Started with CFEngine

The first step toward using CFEngine is getting it installed on at least one machine so that you can start playing with it. CFEngine has fairly simple requirements, so you should be able to build it yourself easily. In this chapter we will go through the process of installing CFEngine on your machine, setting it up, and writing and running your first policy. Don't worry if you do not understand at first glance what all the different pieces mean—the idea of this chapter is to get you going. We will step back in Chapter 3 to examine all the different CFEngine components.

I will mention one concept that you need to understand before we start. Your first CFEngine host will act as the *policy hub*, which is a server from where other CFEngine clients fetch their policy files. If you are just going to start playing with CFEngine, most likely you will be using it on a single host at the beginning, so the hub and the client can be on the same machine. As you grow your CFEngine installation, other machines will connect to the hub as well. Most CFEngine installations use a "star" configuration, with a single hub serving multiple machines. However, this is not a requirement—CFEngine allows you to connect its components in any architecture you desire[1].

Installing CFEngine

Remember that CFEngine exists in two versions: community edition and commercial edition. Therefore, I will describe three options for installing CFEngine:

- Community edition (free), installed from source code
- Community edition (free), installed from a binary package
- Commercial edition, installed from a binary package

---

1. With CFEngine Community there is no difference at all in the software installed on a hub and on a client, just in their configuration. It is easy to convert a client into a hub (and vice versa) by bootstrapping it again with the correct options, as described in "Finishing the Installation and Bootstrapping" on page 16.

Installing the Community Edition from Source

You can download the CFEngine source code in a compressed tar file from *https://cfengine.com/source-code* (as of this writing, the latest released version is 3.3.0). If you are feeling adventurous, you can also fetch the very latest code from the CFEngine git repository by issuing the following command:

```
git clone git://github.com/cfengine/core.git
```

For more details on building the code from git, see the CFEngine Developers Page (*https://cfengine.com/develop*).

CFEngine requires the following packages (with their development-related content, such as header files and libraries):

- OpenSSL (*http://openssl.org/*)
- One of: Qdbm (*http://fallabs.com/qdbm/*) or Tokyo Cabinet (*http://fallabs.com/tokyocabinet/*)
- flex (*http://flex.sourceforge.net/*)
- bison (*http://www.gnu.org/software/bison/*)
- PCRE, the Perl-Compatible Regular Expressions Library (*http://www.pcre.org/*)

 Versions of CFEngine prior to 3.3.0 supported both Berkeley DB and SQLite3 for the database backend, but they were removed due to their technical and performance limitations. The default is now Tokyo Cabinet, and Qdbm is also supported.

Compiling on Linux

Compiling CFEngine on Linux is very easy, as all of the requirements are either included or very easy to install on most major distributions. Depending on your distribution, you may need to explicitly install the development version of each package (for example, in Red Hat Linux you need to install both `openssl` and `openssl-devel`).

Once the required packages are installed, compiling and installing CFEngine is as easy as running the following commands in the CFEngine source directory:

```
./configure
make
sudo make install
```

This will compile CFEngine and install all its binaries and support files under */var/cfengine/*. The binaries will all be located in */var/cfengine/bin/*, so you should add this directory to your `PATH` environment variable to be able to invoke the binaries conveniently.

The configure script by default tries to use Tokyo Cabinet as the DB engine. To use Qdbm, you have to specify it as an option:

```
./configure --with-qdbm
```

You can run *./configure --help* to get a list of all the valid options.

Compiling on Mac OS X

Mac OS X is Unix under the hood, so in principle compiling CFEngine is no different from Linux or other versions of Unix. The main difficulty in installing under OS X is that there is no standard package-management system like in many other versions of Unix, so there are several possible ways of handling the installation of both CFEngine and its prerequisites. The most common package managers for OS X are Fink (*http:// www.finkproject.org/*), MacPorts (*http://www.macports.org/*), and Homebrew (*http:// mxcl.github.com/homebrew/*), and of course you can also compile everything yourself.

As of this writing, Homebrew is the only repository that has the latest version of CFEngine (3.3.0). MacPorts has an older version (3.1.2), and Fink has only CFEngine 2.

Here is how you can compile CFEngine on Mac OS X, depending on your package manager of choice:

 Versions of CFEngine prior to 3.3.0 did not compile natively on Mac OS X 10.7 because the version of BerkeleyDB included with OS X produced a compilation error. With Tokyo Cabinet now being the default, this problem has gone away, but make sure you explicitly specify Tokyo Cabinet if you need to compile an older version of CFEngine.

No package manager
- Download the Tokyo Cabinet distribution from its home page at *http://fallabs .com/tokyocabinet/*.
- Unpack the distribution, then configure and compile it using the commands:

  ```
  ./configure && make && sudo make install
  ```
- Unpack and compile CFEngine using the method described in "Compiling on Linux" on page 12.

Homebrew
- Run *brew update* to update the repository.
- Run *brew install cfengine* to install the latest version from the repository.

MacPorts
- Run *sudo port selfupdate* to update the repository.
- Run *sudo port install tokyocabinet* to install this library.
- Unpack and compile CFEngine using the method described in "Compiling on Linux" on page 12.

Fink
- Run *sudo apt-get update* to update the repository.

- Run *sudo apt-get install tokyocabinet9* to install this library.
- Unpack and compile CFEngine using the method described in "Compiling on Linux" on page 12.

If you use any of the package managers, please make sure you search for CFEngine in the latest version of the repository, in case it has been added since the time of this writing.

Compiling on Windows with cygwin

 These instructions can be used to compile CFEngine 3.2.4 or earlier. In CFEngine 3.3.0, support for Berkeley DB has been deprecated, so you need to use Qdbm to compile it under Windows. However, as of this writing, CFEngine 3.3.0 does not compile cleanly under cygwin. For updates when this situation changes, please check the book's website (*http://cf-learn.info/*).

If you use cygwin (*http://cygwin.com/*) under Windows, it is also very easy to compile CFEngine. Using the cygwin *setup.exe* utility, install the following packages as prerequisites (whenever *setup.exe* asks if you want to install other packages as dependencies, answer "yes"):

- make
- gcc
- libdb4.5
- libdb4.5-devel
- openssl-devel
- libpcre-devel
- bison
- flex

Once this is done, the steps for compiling it are the same as under Unix, except you don't need to use the *sudo* command to install it:

```
$ tar zxvf cfengine-3.3.0.tar.gz
$ cd cfengine-3.3.0
$ ./configure
$ make
$ make install
```

Remember that there is some functionality missing in the community edition under Windows (for example, the userexists() function does not return correct results). If you want full Windows support (including native features like registry editing, etc.) you have to use the commercial edition of CFEngine. But for all the examples in this book, the community edition works just fine.

Installing the Community Edition from Binary Packages

CFEngine AS, the company that provides commercial services and support for CFEngine, also makes available free binary packages of the Community Edition for several popular Linux distributions. You can download these from *https://cfengine.com/inside/myspace*. To access this page you will need to create a free account at *http://cfengine.com/*. Once you download the appropriate package, install it using the corresponding tool for your operating system (for example, *rpm* or *dpkg*).

As easy as it is to compile CFEngine from source, these packages are useful to speed up deployment on multiple machines, or to install it on systems in which you cannot install the development tools and libraries needed to compile it.

Installing the Commercial Edition

If you have purchased the commercial edition of CFEngine, you will get access to the binary packages of CFEngine Nova (or the latest commercial edition) for all the supported operating systems, including a native Windows installer. You will also need to register your CFEngine policy server, so that it can operate with all the full features of the commercial edition.

The policy language in the commercial edition of CFEngine is a strict superset of the Community Edition, so you can start by practicing with the Community Edition, and move to the commercial edition as you gain more experience and need more advanced features, knowing that your existing policies will work just as before.

The current commercial version of CFEngine comes in two packages, called `cfengine-nova` and `cfengine-nova-expansion`. The first one contains the core components of CFEngine and should be installed on all the machines. The second package should be installed only in the *policy hub*, the central host from where clients will fetch their policies, and where the CFEngine graphical console available with Nova is installed.

For example, in an Ubuntu machine that will be the policy server, you can install CFEngine Nova using the following commands:

```
# dpkg --install cfengine-nova_2.1.3-1_x86_64.deb
# dpkg --install cfengine-nova-expansion_2.1.3-1_x86_64.deb
```

For the graphical console to function properly, you need to install other packages as described in the documentation you get with Nova. For example, in an Ubuntu installation, you can install them with the following command:

```
# apt-get install apache2 php5 php5-cli php5-mcrypt php-pear subversion
```

After this, you can continue with the bootstrap process as described next.

Finishing the Installation and Bootstrapping

Depending on your installation method, you may need to finish bootstrapping the system by hand. You need to follow these steps:

1. Run the command */var/cfengine/bin/cf-key*. This will generate a private- and public-key pair for the current host.

   ```
   # /var/cfengine/bin/cf-key
   Making a key pair for cfengine, please wait, this could take a minute...
   ```

   These keys are necessary when operating in a distributed CFEngine environment. This command also sets up under */var/cfengine/* the basic directory structure used by CFEngine. The generated keys will be stored in */var/cfengine/ppkeys/*.

   If the keys already exist (CFEngine-provided binary packages run this command automatically during the installation) you will see the following message:

   ```
   # /var/cfengine/bin/cf-key
   A key file already exists at /var/cfengine/ppkeys/localhost.pub
   ```

2. CFEngine installs its binaries by default in */var/cfengine/bin/*. Some binary packages also copy them to */usr/local/sbin/* to have them in the same directory as other system utilities. If you installed from source, you may want to copy them by hand:

   ```
   # cp /var/cfengine/bin/cf-* /usr/local/sbin/
   ```

    Prior to CFEngine 3.3.0, the opposite held true: the binaries were installed by default under */usr/local/sbin/*, and you had to copy them to */var/cfengine/bin/* so that CFEngine could find them.

3. On the policy hub, CFEngine expects to find its "master files" under */var/cfengine/ masterfiles/*. This is meant to be the master copy of its policy files, from where they will be copied to the work directory (*/var/cfengine/inputs/* by default). If the */var/ cfengine/masterfiles/* directory is empty or nonexistent (this will be the case if you installed from source, or with some of the packages), you need to populate it with the sample *masterfiles* directory from the CFEngine distribution, which normally gets installed in */var/cfengine/share/CoreBase/*:

    Prior to CFEngine 3.3.0, the sample masterfiles were installed under */usr/local/share/cfengine/masterfiles/*.

   ```
   # ls /var/cfengine/masterfiles
   ls: /var/cfengine/masterfiles: No such file or directory
   # cp -Rp /var/cfengine/share/CoreBase /var/cfengine/masterfiles
   # ls /var/cfengine/masterfiles/
   cfengine_stdlib.cf      failsafe.cf        promises.cf
   ```

We will examine these files in detail later on.

4. Finally, CFEngine needs to be "bootstrapped." This means copying the masterfiles to their final working location in */var/cfengine/inputs/* and starting the base *cf-execd* daemon. This process controls the periodic execution of *cf-agent*, which is the one that actually executes the promises in the provided policies (we will look in more detail at the different components in "CFEngine Components" on page 27).

First, find the IP address of your policy server, using the *ifconfig* command (*ipconfig* under Windows). Let's assume it is 192.168.1.141. Then, run the *cf-agent* command with the --bootstrap and the --policy-server options, as shown here:

```
# /var/cfengine/bin/cf-agent --bootstrap --policy-server 192.168.1.141
** CFEngine BOOTSTRAP probe initiated


    @@@
    @@@        CFEngine

  @ @@@ @      CFEngine Core 3.3.0
  @ @@@ @
  @ @@@ @
  @     @
    @@@
    @ @
    @ @
    @ @


 Copyright (C) Cfengine AS 2008-2011

   -> This host is: myhostname
   -> Operating System Type is darwin
   -> Operating System Release is 11.1.0
   -> Architecture = x86_64
   -> Internal soft-class is darwin
   -> No policy failsafe discovered, assume temporary bootstrap vector
   -> No previous policy has been cached on this host
   -> Assuming the policy distribution point at:
      192.168.1.141:/var/cfengine/masterfiles
   -> Attempting to initiate promised autonomous services...


   ** This host recognizes itself as a CFEngine Policy Hub,
   ** with policy distribution and knowledge base.
   -> The system is now converging. Full initialisation and
   -> self-analysis could take up to 30 minutes

 There is no readable input file at ./failsafe.cf
   !!! System error for stat: "No such file or directory"
 cf-agent was not able to get confirmation of promises from cf-promises,
 so going to failsafe
 R: This host assumes the role of policy distribution host
 R:  -> Updated local policy from policy server
 R:  -> Started the server
```

```
    R:  -> Started the scheduler
    -> Bootstrap to 192.168.1.141 completed successfully
```

You can verify the success of this command by looking at the process list. You should see at least the *cf-execd* process, and maybe some others that are started at different times by cf-execd:

```
# ps -ax | grep cf
84284 ??         0:00.22 /var/cfengine/bin/cf-execd
84287 ??         0:00.15 /var/cfengine/bin/cf-serverd
84358 ??         0:00.25 /var/cfengine/bin/cf-monitord
```

If you already have a policy hub running, you should provide its IP address to the --policy-server option when you bootstrap CFEngine on other machines.

Auxiliary Files

The CFEngine distribution includes not only the binaries, but also a large library of documentation and examples. The examples normally get installed in */var/cfengine/share/doc/* (in previous versions they were installed under */usr/local/share/cfengine/* or */usr/local/share/doc/cfengine/*, and can be of big help for getting started. These directories include examples of CFEngine configurations for different tasks and demonstrate the use of different CFEngine constructs. The *examples* directory contains a large number of mostly-self-contained files that demonstrate and exercise different CFEngine abilities.

Your First CFEngine Policy

Now that you have CFEngine installed and running, let us start by writing a first simple policy. If you have finished the bootstrapping process described in "Finishing the Installation and Bootstrapping" on page 16, you can be sure that CFEngine is properly installed. You can also check this by running the following command:

```
$ /var/cfengine/bin/cf-agent -V

  @@@
  @@@        cf-agent

@ @@@ @      CFEngine Core 3.3.0
@ @@@ @
@ @@@ @
@     @
  @@@
  @ @
  @ @
  @ @


Copyright (C) CFEngine AS 2008-2012
See Licensing at http://cfengine.com/3rdpartylicenses
```

For our first policy, let us tackle a task that is simple to explain, yet can be useful in real systems. We will add a line to the /etc/motd file to indicate that CFEngine is running on this machine. And to keep with the tradition, we will also print out a "Hello world!" message to the console when the policy is run.

All CFEngine policies must have a "control body" that contains general configuration and execution information. The only mandatory element in this section is bundlesequence, which tells CFEngine which *bundles* (containers of promises) to execute, and in which order. For our sample policy, we will have a single bundle executed:

```
body common control
{
        bundlesequence => { "edit_motd" };
}
```

This tells CFEngine that upon execution, this policy must run the bundle called edit_motd. Here it is:

```
bundle agent edit_motd ❶
{
  vars:    ❷
      "motd" string => "/etc/motd";

  files:   ❸
      "$(motd)"
        create => "true",
        edit_line => addmessage;

  reports:   ❹
    cfengine::
      "Hello world!";
}
```

This is the part of the policy that tells CFEngine what to do. Here is how it works:

❶ In CFEngine, a bundle of type "agent" (identified by its declaration bundle agent, followed by an arbitrary identifier, in this case edit_motd) could be considered the equivalent of a subroutine, and contains promises that CFEngine evaluates and acts on, if needed. It is split into sections that correspond to different types of promises, which are the lines that start with a word and end with a single colon. In this bundle, we have three sections: vars:, files:, and reports:.

❷ The vars: section is used to declare variables. CFEngine has several variable types, including strings, lists, arrays, and numbers (both integers and floating-point numbers are supported). Here we are declaring a single string value named motd, which contains the path of the file we want to edit. If you are testing this on a system where you don't have root privilege, you should change this path to some file you can edit, for example /tmp/motd.

In a CFEngine policy, everything is expressed as promises, even variable declarations. In this case, "motd" promises to be a string variable containing the value /etc/motd". We will reference this variable later in the policy. In CFEngine, scalar variable references are indicated by a dollar sign followed by the variable name enclosed in either parentheses or braces. Both ${motd} and $(motd) refer to the same variable.

❸ In the files: section we indicate the file-related operations we want to perform. In this case, the promiser is "$(motd)" which expands the motd variable into its value, so the promiser becomes "/etc/motd", telling CFEngine which file to edit.

The rest of the promise, up until the semicolon, is called the *body* of the promise, and is formed by attribute => value pairs, separated by commas. In this case we have two attribute specifications: create => "true" and edit_line => addmessage. The former simply indicates that the file needs to be created if it doesn't exist yet. The latter means that lines in *etc/motd* will be edited according to the specification given by a bundle named addmessage.

Casting this into CFEngine terminology: All *promisers* in the files: section are interpreted by CFEngine as files on the system, so the promise in our sample policy means that the *etc/motd* file *promises* to be edited according to the instructions given by the body of the promise. The value of the edit_line parameter is the name of an edit_line *bundle*. This means that it's not a single value, but rather the name of a separate bundle that specifies the behavior of the edit_line attribute. Here is its definition:

```
bundle edit_line addmessage
{
  insert_lines:
      "This system is managed by CFEngine 3";
}
```

This is another bundle, which means it is also a container of promises, and is also divided in sections. The type of each bundle is given by the second word in its declaration (in this case, edit_line). You can see that the edit_motd bundle had agent as its type, which means it's an "execution" bundle that can be called directly (in this case, from the bundlesequence declaration, although there are other means for executing agent bundles that we will cover later). Thus, the first line assigns the type edit_line to the addmessage bundle, meaning that addmessage can be used only as the value of an edit_line attribute. Additionally, the type of a bundle defines what sections are valid in it, and how the promises in it are interpreted. An edit_line bundle must contain promises that perform edits on a file. In this case, it contains an insert_lines: section, so promises are interpreted as lines to be inserted in the file. The only promise in this bundle is a string that contains the message we want to insert in the file. This promise has no body (the string itself is the promiser, and no additional attributes are given), which means the line will always be inserted into the file, *unless it is there already* (this is default behavior).

In summary, what this means is that the given line will be inserted into *etc/motd* if it's not there already.

---

❹ Finally, the `edit_motd` bundle has a `reports:` section, which is meant to produce output during the execution of the policy. Promises in a `reports:` section indicate messages and how they will be handled. By default, the promised message will be printed to the console. In our case, we will print the message `Hello world!` to the console every single time the policy is executed.

You may notice the additional line `cfengine::` that precedes the message. This is a *class expression*, and tells CFEngine under which conditions the promises that follow it will be executed. In this example, `cfengine` is a class that is defined if the policy is being executed by CFEngine, so it will always be true, and the message will always be printed. But we can use other classes. For example, if you replace `cfengine::` with `Monday::`, the message will be printed only on Mondays. CFEngine defines many classes, such as days of the week, and a policy can define any number of arbitrary classes. We will look at this in much more detail in "Classes and Decision Making" on page 37.

So, let us look at the policy in one piece:

```
body common control
{
        bundlesequence => { "edit_motd" };
}

bundle agent edit_motd
{
  vars:
      "motd" string => "/etc/motd";

  files:
      "$(motd)"
        create => "true",
        edit_line => addmessage;

  reports:
    cfengine::
      "Hello world!";
}

bundle edit_line addmessage
{
  insert_lines:
      "This system is managed by CFEngine 3";
}
```

Type this in and save it to a file, for example *edit_motd_helloworld.cf*. You can then execute it with the following command:

```
# cf-agent -KI -f ./edit_motd_helloworld.cf
 -> Edited file /etc/motd
R: Hello world!
```

The -K option means "Ignore locking constraints during execution," which in practice means "always execute all promises." Normally, CFEngine obeys certain time periods between successive evaluations of the same promise, to avoid overloading the systems. The -K option disables those constraints, and so is useful for testing policies that you may run several times in quick succession. The -I option means "Print basic information about changes made to the system," essentially telling CFEngine to show you the actions that it is taking. If not specified, CFEngine's output is quite terse, limited only to reports explicitly printed by the policies and a few other essential messages. The -f option tells CFEngine to use the specified file as its input. Otherwise it will try to read */var/cfengine/inputs/promises.cf*.

Running CFEngine as a Regular User

Most of the examples in this book are shown running as root, since that is the normal conditions under which CFEngine should be executed to have the privileges necessary to exercise changes to the system. However, during development and testing it is perfectly possible to run CFEngine as a regular user. When you run it like this, CFEngine does not look under */var/cfengine/* for its input files, rather it looks under *$HOME/.cfagent/*, so if you run cf-agent without specifying an input file, it will try to read *$HOME/.cfagent/inputs/promises.cf*.

Now examine the /etc/motd file, and you will see that a string like the following has been added to it:

```
This system is managed by CFEngine 3
```

If you run the command again, the output changes:

```
# cf-agent -KI -f ./first_cfengine_policy.cf
R: Hello world!
```

The file already contains the message, so it is not edited again. Now try editing it by hand and removing or modifying the existing line. If you run cf-agent again, the message will reappear.

Congratulations! You have written and executed your first CFEngine policy. This is very basic operation, but the structure that we have seen is very similar to that of any CFEngine policy, and allows enough flexibility and expressibility to tackle the most complex configuration operations.

## CHAPTER 3

CFEngine Basics

In this chapter we will take a more detailed look at the basic concepts behind CFEngine, including its theoretical foundation, the syntax and constructs of its policy language, and some unique aspects of its behavior. I will also point you to some of the many online resources available for learning and improving your CFEngine skills.

Basic Principles

One of CFEngine's unique characteristics is that it is built upon predefined, solid theoretical and behavioral principles. These principles guide the design and implementation of all the CFEngine components and of its policy language, and ensure that the behavior of those components remains consistent. These principles are: desired-state configuration, a minimum base set of native operations, promise theory, and convergent configuration. Let us look at them in more detail.

Desired-State Configuration

CFEngine is different from many other automation mechanisms in that you do not need to tell it what to do. Instead, you specify the state in which you wish the system to be, and CFEngine will automatically decide the actions to take to reach the desired state, or as close to it as possible. In programming language terms, we say that the CFEngine policy language is *declarative*, as opposed to *imperative*.

These are some examples of the things that you can express to CFEngine as desired states:

- "Make sure file */etc/ssh/sshd_config* contains the line `UseDNS no`"
- "Make sure user `mysql` exists/does not exist"
- "Make sure process `httpd` is (not) running"

At a higher level of abstraction, you can encapsulate CFEngine operations and express high-level desired states:

- "Make sure all web servers have Apache installed"
- "Make sure all root accounts have the same, centrally-designated password"
- "Make sure parameters UseDNS and PermitRootLogin are disabled on all *sshd* configurations, except on servers dbsrv01 and dbsrv02, where PermitRootLogin should be enabled"

And at an even higher level, you can express top-level desired states like these:

- "Configure host dbsrv01 as a database server"
- "Create a new cluster of VMs to use as web servers"

Of course, in reality things are not so simple. At some point, CFEngine needs to know what specific changes to make to the system, and how to make them.

Basic CFEngine Operations

These are some of the basic operations that CFEngine natively knows how to perform:

- Extract information from the system itself about its current state and configuration.
- Inspect and modify the contents of text files.
- Check for and manipulate file permissions and ownerships.
- Check for existence of processes running in the system.
- Check for existence of users in the system.
- Run programs and check their exit status.
- Manipulate packages installed on the system.

The commercial version of CFEngine has some additional capabilities, including the following:

- Check and manipulate the Windows registry, event logs, and services.
- Query and manipulate databases, access LDAP, and interact with virtual machines.
- Examine and manipulate file Access Control Lists (ACLs) in systems that support them.
- Manipulate virtual machines on several different platforms.

These operations are sufficient to perform most configuration tasks on a system. At the lowest possible level, CFEngine contains functional specifications of how to make changes to the system. At the highest level, however, you declare what you want as shown in "Desired-State Configuration" on page 23, and leave the details to CFEngine.

CFEngine ships with some built-in libraries that perform more advanced operations using these basic capabilities, and you can also build your own libraries to perform custom checks and activities.

Promise Theory

CFEngine 3 works on top of a theoretical model called *Promise Theory* (*http://research .iu.hio.no/promises.php*). This theory models the behavior of autonomous agents in an environment without central authority, based only on promises of behavior made by each agent, and shows that even without central control, the system can converge to a stable state.

Promise Theory underlays one of the basic tenets of CFEngine: voluntary cooperation. In CFEngine, each system participates voluntarily, makes promises only about its own behavior (if you think about it, it makes no sense for a system to make promises about someone else's behavior), and cannot be forced to accept commands or information from any external entities. This gives CFEngine very strong security properties, since it means that CFEngine running on a host cannot be coerced into modifying its behavior according to some external influence. It may *choose* to do so (for example, by getting policies from a central server), but unlike many other configuration management systems, CFEngine does not require you to open a command channel through which each host can be given instructions (you can do it, and this allows the server to "ping" clients so that they run their policies before their scheduled time, or to query them for information, but never to perform arbitrary actions or commands).

A promise is simply a declaration of *intent*, a model of the desired state of the promiser. A promise does not imply that the desired state will be reached in the next iteration (or ever), but implies a capability for verifying whether the promise has been satisfied. Through this seemingly simple characteristic, promise theory allows CFEngine to deal with a crucial aspect of systems management: operational uncertainty. Systems are under constant change, both intentional (changing requirements, changing software, changing user behavior) and accidental (disconnected network connections, disappearing resources, software crashes) and have to react to it, often with incomplete information. Promise theory allows CFEngine to deal with these conditions in a resilient fashion.

Promise Theory was developed initially as the foundation for CFEngine's behavior (in fact, the policy language in CFEngine 3 was redesigned to reflect this theory), but it has found more general applications in Computer Science and in other disciplines such as Economics and Organization.

According to Promise Theory, everything in CFEngine 3 is a promise, with specifications of what to do if the promise is already satisfied, if the promise was not satisfied but could be fixed, if the promise was not satisfied and could not be fixed, etc. Table 3-1 shows some examples of promises you could find in a CFEngine policy, and of the possible actions CFEngine could take automatically if the promise is not kept.

Table 3-1. Examples of objects (promisers), promises, and repair actions in CFEngine

Promiser	Promises to...	If not currently kept, CFEngine will...
A variable	...hold a certain value of a certain type.	...store the appropriate value in the variable.
A file	...have certain characteristics (permissions, ownership, ACLs, etc.).	...set the desired properties on the file.
A file	...exist and to have certain content.	...create the file if needed, modify its content (add, remove or edit lines) to match the desired state.
A user account	...exist and have certain characteristics (home directory, group, etc.)	...create the user account with the desired characteristics.
A process	...be running on the system.	...run the appropriate command to create the process.
A shell command	...have been executed.	...execute the command and collect its output and exit status.
A directory on the policy hub	...provide access to its content to certain clients.	...reconfigure its access rules to permit or block the access as desired.
An output message	...be generated when certain conditions arise, with a certain frequency and in a certain format.	...produce the appropriate message.

When a promise is not already satisfied (e.g., a file does not exist as it should), CFEngine will take the necessary actions to fix it, according to both its built-in rules and any additional promises declared in the policy.

Depending on the current state of the system with respect to a given promise, on the actions that CFEngine took when evaluating a promise, and on the result of those actions, CFEngine defines the following promise states:

Promise kept
> The state of the system was already as described by the promise, so no action had to be taken.

Promise repaired
> The state of the system was not as required by the promise, so CFEngine took the appropriate actions, and repaired the system state to match the requirements of the promise.

Repair failed
> Repair actions were attempted by CFEngine, but they failed for some reason (for example, lack of permissions to edit a file).

Repair denied
> Repair actions were attempted by CFEngine, but they failed due to lack of access to some resource. (In the current version of CFEngine, this status is set only when CFEngine fails to change the owner or BSD flags of a file, or when it fails to *touch* it.

Repair timeout

>Repair actions were attempted by CFEngine but took too long to execute, and CFEngine cancelled the operation.

A CFEngine policy is constructed out of individual promises that get executed in certain order, and that can interact with other promises. After a promise is evaluated (executed), you can determine its state and act based on it, triggering further actions such as reporting, command execution, or evaluation of other promises.

Convergent Configuration

One of CFEngine's basic principles is *convergent configuration*. This means that you don't have to leave the system in the desired state on the first pass. Instead, you make changes incrementally, getting closer to the objective every time, independently of the starting state of the system. A CFEngine policy may not leave the system completely configured on the first pass, but at least it will make some changes. On subsequent passes, it will continue to make changes, eventually bringing it as close as possible to the desired state.

One advantage of convergent configuration, and of the declarative nature of CFEngine, is that you do not need to know the current state of the system in order to correct it. If the system is already in the desired state, a correctly written CFEngine policy will do nothing. If it's not, CFEngine will iteratively make discrete changes to bring it closer to the ideal, taking only the necessary actions to correct the existing deviations.

In order to carry out convergent configuration, CFEngine performs three passes over its policy. During each pass, all the promises in the policy are evaluated. There may be some promises that cannot be evaluated until the second or third pass due to dependencies between different components of the policy, so the multiple passes help CFEngine bring things to a convergent state as soon as possible.

CFEngine Components

A CFEngine installation contains multiple components that perform different, specific functions, as shown in Figure 3-1. Dotted lines represent components that execute others, solid lines represent communication among components, and bold lines indicate data flow.

Let's look in more detail at the functionality and role of each one of these components.

cf-agent

>This is the "instigator of change," as described in the CFEngine documentation. *cf-agent* is the program that evaluates policies and acts on them, making any necessary changes to the system. *cf-agent* is normally started directly (for example, we have been running it directly from the command line to test the policies in this book), or by one of two higher-level commands: *cf-execd* (as a mechanism for

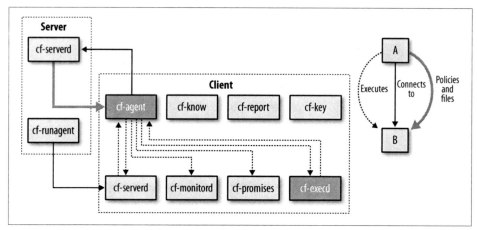

Figure 3-1. CFEngine components and their relationships

starting it at regular intervals) or *cf-serverd* (in response to the *cf-runagent* command executed from a different host). Note that depending on its policies, *cf-agent* can in turn be responsible for restarting *cf-execd*, *cf-serverd* or *cf-monitord* if they have stopped for any reason (in addition, *cf-promises* is used by *cf-agent* to validate its policies before attempting to run them).

By default, *cf-agent* will attempt to run */var/cfengine/inputs/promises.cf* (more precisely, the file found by expanding the variable in `$(sys.workdir)/inputs/promises.cf`) when invoked, unless a different file is specified using the `-f` command-line option. If the filename executed produces an error, *cf-agent* will try to run */var/cfengine/inputs/failsafe.cf*. The idea is for *failsafe.cf* to be a barebones policy that does little more than try to restore the CFEngine policies to a working state. Normally *failsafe.cf* will attempt to update the local policies from the policy hub, and it may also try to start *cf-execd* and *cf-monitord* to have at least a minimal CFEngine infrastructure running.

cf-execd

This process executes *cf-agent* in a periodic basis, collecting its output, and potentially emailing it somewhere. By default, *cf-execd* runs *cf-agent* every five minutes, but you can modify its behavior using an `executor control` body. For example:

```
body executor control
{
    any::

        splaytime  => "10";
        mailto     => "cfengine@example.org";
        mailfrom   => "cfengine@$(sys.host).example.org";
        smtpserver => "mail.example.org";

        schedule => { "Min00_05", "Min30_35" };
```

}

In this case, the `schedule` attribute tells *cf-execd* to only run *cf-agent* every 30 minutes (more precisely, whenever either the `Min00_05` or `Min30_35` classes are enabled, which would be the case between 00-05 and 30-35 minutes of every hour). The `splaytime` parameter tells *cf-execd* that the execution could be delayed up to 10 minutes (this is useful in large installations to prevent all the clients from connecting to the server at once). The `mailto`, `mailfrom` and `smtpserver` attributes determine how email reports will be sent.

It is common for *cf-execd* to be the one process started by the operating system (for example, through a cron job) when the system starts. *cf-execd* then runs *cf-agent*, which makes sure through the appropriate policies that *cf-execd*, *cf-monitord*, and *cf-serverd* are running in the background, if needed.

cf-serverd
> This component implements server functionality in CFEngine—the ability to listen for connections from clients and serve files to them. *cf-serverd* also has the ability to listen for connections from the *cf-runagent* process in other hosts, and according to its configuration, respond by executing *cf-agent* locally (this is the one reason why you may want to run *cf-serverd* on CFEngine clients: if you want the policy hub to be able to remotely instruct clients to run *cf-agent*). We will look in more detail at the *cf-serverd* configuration in "Clients and Servers" on page 57. *cf-serverd* listens on port TCP/5308, and this is the only port that needs to be open for the clients to be able to communicate with the server.

cf-runagent
> Invokes *cf-agent* on remote hosts so that they evaluate their policies. This is the only form of control a remote machine may exercise over another in CFEngine. We will talk more about this in "CFEngine Remote Execution Using cf-runagent" on page 63.

cf-key
> This is one of the first commands you run when installing CFEngine on a new host. It creates a cryptographic key pair for the current host, which is used for authentication when communicating with the policy hub or any other CFEngine server.

cf-monitord
> This process is intended to run continuously in the background. It collects statistical information about different aspects of the system and makes it available to *cf-agent* through the special `mon` variable context. Some examples of the information collected by *cf-monitord* are the numbers of users with active processes in the system (`mon.value_users`), free space in the root disk partition (`mon.value_disk free`), and kernel load average (`mon.value_loadavg`). For most values *cf-monitord* also keeps a running average and the standard deviation (for example, `mon.av_loadvg` and `mon.dev_loadavg`).

cf-report
> Extracts and reports information about CFEngine's behavior, including promise handling statistics (promises kept, repaired, and failed), types of promises, etc.

cf-know
> Allows the processing of knowledge-management promises in the policy, and the production of knowledge maps from them. This is an advanced topic that we will not cover in this book.

A First Example

Let's consider the simple case of modifying the configuration of an *ssh* server. At the top level, we need to make sure the sshd service is up and running. With CFEngine, we can simply write the following:

```
services:
  "ssh";
```

This will by default enable and make sure the service is running, on any operating system. If we wanted to make sure the service is not running, we would simply need to write:

```
services:
  "ssh" service_policy => "stop";
```

 A new model for `services:` promises was introduced in CFEngine 3.3.0, which allows greatly simplified service management as shown above. In previous versions, you needed to manipulate the services through a combination of `processes:` and `commands:` promises.

Now, let's go down a level and change the configuration of the ssh daemon. Traditionally, we would do this sort of task with a shell script. The following snippet from a shell script is intended to add a line to */etc/ssh/sshd_config* to prevent root logins:

```
echo "PermitRootLogin no" >> /etc/ssh/sshd_config
```

As is, this code will add a new line to the file every time it runs. It assumes that the file does not contain the line already. Of course, you can add checks for this, but the code quickly becomes unreadable:

```
(grep -iq 'PermitRootLogin' /etc/ssh/sshd_config ||
  echo "PermitRootLogin no" >> /etc/ssh/sshd_config) &&
  sed -i 's/^.*PermitRootLogin.*$/PermitRootLogin no/;' /etc/ssh/sshd_config
```

This snippet uses the *grep* command to determine if the file already contains the `PermitRootLogin` string, and based on the result either adds the corresponding line or uses the *sed* command to edit the existing line.

Compare this with the equivalent CFEngine declaration:

```
files:
    "/etc/ssh/sshd_config"
        comment => "Ensure root login is disallowed",
        edit_line => replace_or_add(".*PermitRootLogin.*", "PermitRootLogin no");
```

The CFEngine policy will add the line only if it is not there already. Additionally, you can see that CFEngine rules allow comments as rule attributes. These comments can be made available as the policy executes, allowing administrators to better understand and debug the actions taken by CFEngine.

Rules in CFEngine can be as detailed or as high-level as you wish. For example, you could generalize the SSH configuration file mechanism and express it like this (and we will look into the details of how to do this in "Editing /etc/sshd_config" on page 78):

```
vars:
    # SSHD configuration to set
    "sshd[Protocol]"        string => "2";
    "sshd[X11Forwarding]"   string => "yes";
    "sshd[UseDNS]"          string => "no";
    "sshd[PermitRootLogin]" string => "no";

files:
    "/etc/ssh/sshd_config"
        handle    => "sshd_config",
        comment   => "Set sshd configuration",
        edit_line => set_config_values("sshd"),
        classes   => if_repaired("restart_sshd");

commands:
    restart_sshd::
        "/etc/init.d/sshd reload"
            handle  => "sshd_restart",
            comment => "Restart sshd if the configuration file was modified";
```

This CFEngine policy allows you to define arbitrary configuration parameters in the sshd array defined at the top (in the vars: section), which will be applied by the files: section by modifying or adding only those parameters that need to be fixed. Finally, *sshd* will be restarted only if any changes were made. In other words, the promise of having the right parameters in the file could be satisfied just by checking that they're set properly already (the "Promise kept" state described earlier), so the restart will take place only in the "Promise repaired" state.

Let's go back to our description of promises, to start figuring out what is happening in this policy. The vars: section is simply variable declarations—in this case, an array indexed by configuration parameter names, and containing the values of each parameter. In the files: section, the *etc/ssh/sshd_config* file promises to have its content edited according to the specifications contained in the set_config_values() function (called *bundles* in CFEngine terminology), and to set the restart_sshd class if the file needed to be repaired (i.e. modified to satisfy the promise). Finally, in the commands: section, the command to restart *sshd* promises to run only if the restart_sshd class is set (if this class is set, it means that the file was modified, so the daemon needs to be restarted for the changes to take effect).

Not shown in this example is the `set_config_values()` bundle, which is part of the CFEngine Standard Library, and which takes care of the actual editing of the file to set the desired parameters, using the built-in file-editing primitives in CFEngine. We will examine this bundle in detail in "Editing /etc/sshd_config" on page 78.

CFEngine allows you to express configuration policies at the level of abstraction you wish, leaving lower-level details out of sight but available when you need them. Now, let's take a more detailed look at the syntax of a CFEngine policy.

CFEngine Policy Structure

The syntax of the CFEngine 3 configuration files is very uniform, since everything is a promise. In general, every element in a CFEngine policy has the following structure:

```
promise_type:
  class_expression::
    "promiser" -> { "promisee1", "promiseeX" }
        attribute1 => value1,
        attributeX => valueX;
        ...
```

The values that *promise_type* can have depend on the type of container in which the promise is stored (and we will look at them in detail in "Containers" on page 41). The value of *promise_type* determines how the *"promiser"* is interpreted, which *attributes* are valid and how their corresponding *values* are used. The attribute values can be either constant values, variables of the types described in "Data Types and Variables in CFEngine" on page 33, or container names as described in "Containers" on page 41. The type of allowed values is fixed for each attribute.

The *promisees* are optional and, if specified, contain references to other promises that depend on the current one, and are used for documentation. In this way, we can specify which promises affect others. CFEngine has the ability to produce reports that include this information. Note that specifying promisees has no effect on the execution order of the policy, they are merely for informational purposes.

The *class_expression*, if specified, allows the promise to be conditionally executed depending on the value of the expression. We will look at them in detail in "Classes and Decision Making" on page 37.

Depending on the type of promise, almost all elements of this syntax, except for the *promise_type* and the *promiser*, are optional. For example, to unconditionally execute a command, we would simply state it like this:

```
commands:
    "/bin/ls /";
```

In this case `commands:` is the promise type, and specifies that the promisers in the following section are to be interpreted as commands to execute. The promiser, `"/bin/ls /"` indicates the command to execute. Since no attributes are specified, the command will always be executed and its output reported by CFEngine.

Data Types and Variables in CFEngine

CFEngine supports different data types: scalars can be strings, integers or floating-point numbers; lists contain an ordered set of scalars, and arrays contain sets of values indexed by arbitrary strings. These data types can be used as constant values or be stored in variables.

Variable declarations

Variables in CFEngine are declared in the `vars:` section (they are promises of type `vars:`) of a bundle. `vars:` is one of the common promise types (along with `classes:` and `reports:`) that can be included in any type of bundle. `vars:` promises adhere to the common structure described in "CFEngine Policy Structure" on page 32, which in this case is interpreted as follows:

```
vars:
    "variable"
      type => value;
```

The promiser is the name of the variable in quotes. The type of the variable is given as an attribute, and its value indicates the value to store in the variable. Normally you write the whole declaration in a single line for brevity, like this:

```
vars:
    "name"   string => "Diego";
    "year"   int    => "2011";
    "colors" slist  => { "red", "green", "blue" };
```

The only valid attribute in variable declarations besides the type is `policy`, which defines whether a variable can be modified. By default, all variables in CFEngine are defined as constants, and you will get an error if you try to assign a new value to a previously-defined variable. Usually, you'll have no need to change a variable. But you can do so if you set `policy` to `"overridable"` or `"free"` (they are synonyms).

Let us now look at the details of the different data types available in CFEngine.

Strings

Strings in CFEngine are declared using the `string` type. String values must always be enclosed by single or double quotes (there is no difference in their behavior). If you need to include a double quote in a double-quoted string, you need to precede it with a backslash (and viceversa for single-quoted strings). You can create multiline strings simply by splitting them across multiple lines. To reference a string variable (and any scalar variable), you need to enclose the variable name in parentheses or curly braces, and precede them with a dollar sign.

You can interpolate variables into a string simply by referencing them inside the string. The following example shows some examples of strings:

```
body common control
{
        bundlesequence => { "test" };
}

bundle agent test
{
  vars:
        "s1" string => "one";
        "s2" string => "this
is a
multine string";
        "s3" string => "with \"quotes\"";

    reports:
      cfengine::
        "s1 = $(s1)";
        "s2 = $(s2)";
        "s3 = $(s3)";
}
```

If you save this short policy into a file and run it, you will get the following output:

```
$ cf-agent -KI -f ./vars_string_examples.cf
R: s1 = one
R: s2 = this
is a
multine string
R: s3 = with "quotes"
```

Note that the strings in the reports: section adhere to the same rules, and contain the interpolated values of the declared variables.

Numbers

CFEngine supports both integers and floating-point numbers, denoted by the int and real types. Note that numeric values are also given as strings in CFEngine, but they are checked for validity before they are stored in the variable. For integers, CFEngine supports the suffixes k, m. and g to represent powers of 10 (that is, 1000, etc.), and the prefixes K, M and G to represent powers of 2 (that is, 1024, etc.). Real numbers can be specified in decimal or exponential notation. For example:

```
body common control
{
        bundlesequence => { "test" };
}

bundle agent test
```

```
{
  vars:
      "i1" int => "25";
      "i2" int => "10k";
      "i3" int => "10K";
      "r1" real => "1.2";
      "r2" real => "10e-5";

  reports:
    cfengine::
      "i1 = $(i1)";
      "i2 = $(i2)";
      "i3 = $(i3)";
      "r1 = $(r1)";
      "r2 = $(r2)";
}
```

Produces the following output:

```
$ cf-agent -KI -f ./vars_num_examples.cf
R: i1 = 25
R: i2 = 10000
R: i3 = 10240
R: r1 = 1.200000
R: r2 = 0.000100
```

Lists

CFEngine supports ordered lists of any of the scalar types: lists of strings (slist), lists of integers (ilist) and lists of reals (rlist). In all cases, the values have to be specified as strings, but they are interpreted and validated according to the declared type. You can assign and store lists across variables of different types, as long as the values are compatible. This means you can always assign an ilist or an rlist into an slist, but you can assign an slist into an ilist or rlist only if it contains valid values according to the type of the destination variable.

You can refer to list variables by using an at-sign (@) before the variable name. By doing this you can pass the whole list to a function that expects a list argument. You can also specify a list as part of another list value, and it will be expanded in place. The following example illustrates these points:

```
body common control
{
        bundlesequence => { "test" };
}

bundle agent test
{
  vars:
      "l1" ilist => { "1", "2", "3" };
      "l2" rlist => { "1.0", "2.0", "3.0" };
      "l3" slist => { "one", "two", "three", @(l1), @(l2) };

  reports:
```

```
    cfengine::
        "l3 = $(l3)";
}
```

When you run it you get the following output:

```
$ cf-agent -KI -f ./vars_list_examples.cf
R: l3 = one
R: l3 = two
R: l3 = three
R: l3 = 1
R: l3 = 2
R: l3 = 3
R: l3 = 1.0
R: l3 = 2.0
R: l3 = 3.0
```

Both @(l1) and @(l2) are being expanded inside @(l3), so that its final value is this:

```
{ "one", "two", "three", "1", "2", "3", "1.0", "2.0", "3.0" }
```

In this example we are also using CFEngine implicit looping by referring to the @(l3) array as a scalar $(l3). See "Looping in CFEngine" on page 53 for a full explanation of how this works.

Arrays

Arrays are sets of values indexed by a string (they are commonly called *hashes* in other programming languages). Array elements can contain scalars, lists or other arrays, even within the same array.

In CFEngine, arrays are declared element by element, as if they were regular variables, except their name contains the index surrounded by brackets. There is no shortcut for declaring the whole array in a single step. There are certain functions that operate on arrays, such as getindices() and getvalues(), and they receive as argument the name of the array as a string. For example, we could use an array to store user account information:

```
body common control
{
        bundlesequence => { "test" };
}

bundle agent test
{
  vars:
        "user[name]"                string => "zamboni";
        "user[fullname][first]"     string => "Diego";
        "user[fullname][last]"      string => "Zamboni";
        "user[dirs]"                slist => { "/home/zamboni",
                                               "/tmp/zamboni",
                                               "/export/home/zamboni" };

        "fields"    slist => getindices("user");
```

```
    "userfields" slist => getindices("user[fullname]");

reports:
  cfengine::
    "user fields = $(fields)";
    "account name = $(user[name])";
    "$(userfields) name = $(user[fullname][$(userfields)])";
    "user dir = $(user[dirs])";
}
```

This example is intentionally contrived to show how you can store different data types in an array. Note how @(fields) is being automatically populated by getindices() based on the indices declared for the user array. In other words, the statement:

```
    "fields"    slist => getindices("user");
```

creates a variable named fields that refers to a list of three strings taken from the indices: name, fullname, and dirs. The list can then be used to loop through the user array, like before. Additionally, @(userfields) is being populated with the indices of the array stored in user[fullname]:

```
    "userfields" slist => getindices("user[fullname]");
```

Finally, observe that user[dirs] contains a list of strings, and we are looping over that list as we would over a regular list variable (such as @(fields) or @(userfields) in this example) by referencing it as a scalar:

```
    "user dir = $(user[dirs])";
```

Here is its output:

```
$ cf-agent -KI -f ./vars_array_examples2.cf
R: user fields = name
R: user fields = fullname
R: user fields = dirs
R: account name = zamboni
R: first name = Diego
R: last name = Zamboni
R: user dir = /home/zamboni
R: user dir = /tmp/zamboni
R: user dir = /export/home/zamboni
```

Classes and Decision Making

Classes are the key to controlling flow and making decisions in a CFEngine policy. In CFEngine, classes are named attributes that can be either *true* (the class is defined) or *false* (the class is undefined). Classes can represent any attribute about the system, information that is known (true) or unknown (false), or any condition that you want to indicate in the policy. They can be volatile (they stop existing as soon as the current CFEngine run is over) or persistent for a period of time you define. While many important classes are predefined by CFEngine (*hard classes*), you can define others for your particular needs (*soft classes*).

Hard classes

These are defined automatically by CFEngine when it runs, and represent mainly information about the system or the current environment that is discovered by CFEngine. Examples of hard classes include:

- Host information (e.g., class doomsday would be defined if the hostname of the machine where *cf-agent* is running is "doomsday" and class ipv4_192_168_1_2 would be defined if the host's IP address is 192.168.1.2).

- Time information (e.g., class Hr5 would be set if CFEngine is running between 5 and 6 AM, class Min15_20 is defined if it is currently between minutes 15 and 20 of the hour, and class Mon would be set if it's Monday).

- Operating system information (e.g., linux would be set on any Linux system, and suse_9 would be set if the Linux distribution is SuSE 9).

To see the full list of hard classes defined on a particular system, run the following command (example output from my Mac at this moment, 11:52PM on a Friday, one line was cut for length):

```
$ cf-promises -v | grep Defined
cf3> -> Defined classes = { 141_1_168_192_in_addr_arpa 192_168_1_141
64_bit Day23 Evening Friday GMT_Hr4 Hr23 Hr23_Q4 Lcycle_1 Min50_55
Min51 PK_MD5_875d88dcda0fa406d197ca8a2a867842 Q4 September Yr2011
any cfengine cfengine_3 cfengine_3_2 cfengine_3_2_1 common
community_edition compiled_on_darwin11_1_0 darwin darwin_11_1_0
darwin_x86_64 darwin_x86_64_11_1_0
darwin_x86_64_11_1_0_Darwin_Kernel_Version_11_1_0__Tue_Jul_26_16_07...
ipv4_192 ipv4_192_168 ipv4_192_168_1 ipv4_192_168_1_141 net_iface_en0
net_iface_en1 net_iface_fw0 net_iface_gif0 net_iface_lo0 net_iface_p2p0
net_iface_stf0 undefined_domain verbose_mode x86_64 yemi }
```

Soft classes

These are defined by the policy during its execution. For example, a class could be defined in the following cases:

- Depending on whether a certain file exists. In this example, we set the devel_host class if the */var/sitedata/devel_host.flag* file exists, using the built-in fileexists() function to perform the check:

```
classes:
    "devel_host" expression => fileexists("/var/sitedata/devel_host.flag");
```

Setting a class like this might be useful, for example, to establish whether certain executable programs or other capabilities are present on a system before invoking them, or to apply different configurations to the system.

- As a Boolean expression of other classes. In this example, test_host will be defined if any of testhost1, testhost2, or testhost3 classes is defined. These might be the hostnames of the machines in which you want the test_host class to be defined:

```
classes:
    "test_host" or => { "testhost1", "testhost2", "testhost3"};
```

Setting a class like this might be useful to run certain operations on certain systems—tests in this case.

- As an indication that changes were made to a file. In this example, if any changes are made to the */etc/ssh/sshd_config* file by the `edit_line` attribute, CFEngine would consider the promise as *repaired*, in which case the `restart_sshd` class will be defined:

```
files:
  "/etc/ssh/sshd_config"
    edit_line => set_config_values("sshd"),
    classes   => if_repaired("restart_sshd");
```

Setting a class like this might be useful to keep track of the state of the system, and make sure that CFEngine follows up on an operation during its next pass.

Note that classes can be explicitly defined in a `classes:` section, but as you can see in the third example, they can also be defined by the common `classes` attribute, which you can use in all promises to set or unset classes based on the result of the promise. Several `classes` bodies are predefined in the CFEngine standard library, including `if_repaired()`, `if_ok()`, `if_notkept()`, `if_else()` and `always()`

Classes and Contexts

The term "class" is most commonly associated with Object-Oriented Programming. To avoid confusion, the CFEngine developers have decided to rename "classes" to "contexts". This change has not taken place yet in the CFEngine code, but you may encounter this term in use by the time you read this. In any case, it is likely that the CFEngine 3 policy language will retain compatibility with "classes" for a very long time, to avoid breaking existing policies.

Apart from defining classes, you need a way to act on them. This is what the *class_expression* shown in "CFEngine Policy Structure" on page 32 is for. A class expression in CFEngine is a boolean expression constructed with class names and the boolean operators AND (& or .), OR (|) and NOT (!). Parenthesis can be used to group parts of the expression. When a line ends with a double colon, it is evaluted as a class expression. Only if the class expression is true are the lines that follow evaluated. The following are examples of valid class expressions:

```
linux::       True if the linux class is defined
reboot_needed.linux::    True if both reboot_needed and linux are defined
reboot_needed.!(linux|windows)::    True if reboot_needed is defined and neither linux nor windows
                                                                 are defined

any::    The any class is always defined, so whatever follows will always be evaluated
```

Additionally, you can use the `ifvarclass` attribute in most promise types to condition the evaluation of one promise to the result of the included class expression. For example, the following two promises are equivalent:

```
commands:
  # First command is conditioned by the ifvarclass attribute
  "/usr/sbin/shutdown -r now"
    ifvarclass => "linux";
  # Second command is conditioned by the class expression before it
  linux::
    "/usr/sbin/shutdown -r now";
```

The `ifvarclass` attribute allows you to place a condition around a single promise. It has the advantage of specifying the class expression as a string, which means you can use variables in the class expression, and they will be expanded before evaluating the expression. This allows a lot of flexibility in the types of conditions that you can use. For example, you can construct class names on the fly using variables:

```
body common control
{
        bundlesequence => { "test" };
}

bundle agent test
{
  vars:
      "words" slist => { "apple", "darwin", "table", "linux" };
  reports:
    cfengine::
      "Class $(words) is defined"
        ifvarclass => "$(words)";
      "Class $(words) is not defined"
        ifvarclass => "!$(words)";
}
```

In this example, the `reports:` section is looping through all the strings in the @(words) list (see "Looping in CFEngine" on page 53), and the corresponding message is printed depending on whether the class named after the current value is defined. Note how the class expression for the second report ("not defined") includes the NOT character at the beginning. Here is its output on a Mac:

```
$ cf-agent -KI -f ./ifvarclass_examples.cf
R: Class darwin is defined
R: Class apple is not defined
R: Class table is not defined
R: Class linux is not defined
```

Class expressions can also be used to define other classes using the `expression` attribute in a `classes:` promise. For example, the `test_host` class shown above could also be defined like this:

```
classes:
  "test_host" expression => "testhost1|testhost2|testhost3";
```

Finally, classes can be made persistent, even across invocations of *cf-agent*, by using the `persistence` attribute in the class declaration. Its value should be the length of time, in minutes, for which the class should retain its value after being evaluated. This can be useful if the class value is the result of a time-consuming or otherwise expensive operation, to avoid recomputation every time *cf-agent* runs.

Note that setting a class as persistent does not mean it will not be reevaluated every time cf-agent runs, only that its previous value will be available during the persistence period. To avoid unnecessary reevaluation, the usual practice is to use a "flag class" with the same persistence period. For example:

```
bundle agent test
{
  classes:
    !cache_is_active::
      "line_exists"    expression => regline(".*foo.*", "/tmp/test_data.txt"),
        persistence => "1";
      "cache_is_active" expression => "any",
        persistence => "1";
  reports:
    line_exists::
      "Line exists in file";
    !line_exists::
      "Line does not exist in file";
}
```

In this case, we are using `cache_is_active` as the "flag class" to indicate whether we should recompute the value of `line_class` (which would, arguably, be a very costly class to compute. In this case we are using `regline()` to look for a line containing "foo" in the file */tmp/test_data.txt*). In the `classes:` section, we evaluate the classes only when `cache_is_active` is not defined. In this case, we set `cache_is_active` unconditionally (using the special expression `"any"`), and set `line_exists` depending on the result of the function, both with the same persistence period. This means that within one minute, no matter how many times *cf-agent* executes, the classes will not be reevaluated and their cached values will be reported. You can test this behavior in the previous example by running it, then editing the file, and observing that the changes are not detected until a minute has passed since the last execution. In deployment, this can be extremely useful to limit reevaluation of complex or costly class expressions whose values change slowly or infrequently.

Containers

CFEngine promises can grow quite complex, so it would not be very scalable simply to list promises back to back. For this reason, and to promote reusability, CFEngine groups its syntax elements into two types of containers: *bundles* and *bodies*.

Bundles

Bundles are the most general and powerful grouping mechanism. They are the only elements that can contain promises. A bundle can contain many promises, possibly separated into sections. The structure described at the beginning of "CFEngine Policy

Structure" on page 32 can be contained only inside a bundle. Bundles are defined as follows:

```
bundle type name(arguments)
{
  promise_type:
    class_expression:
      promise
      ...
}
```

The *name* of the bundle is an arbitrary string that you can use to identify it. The *type* of the bundle has to be one of the CFEngine-recognized types, and it defines the semantics of the bundle (that is, how are the promises in it interpreted), as well as the promise type sections it can contain. All bundles can receive an arbitrary number of arguments. If no arguments are needed, the parenthesis are optional.

The bundle types defined by CFEngine are:

agent
> Bundles of type agent are "executable" bundles that can be called from the main bundlesequence declaration, or as method calls in the methods: section of another agent bundle. In this respect they could be compared to subroutines in other programming languages. They are the most extensive and powerful type of bundle, and the ones that actually implement any changes that we want to make in the system. These bundles can contain the following promise types:
>
> - commands: to specify commands to be executed
> - files: to edit and manipulate files
> - methods: to call other agent bundles
> - packages: to query and manipulate software packages in the system
> - processes: to query and manipulate running processes
> - storage: to query and configure file systems
> - services: to configure system services in Unix-like systems
>
> In addition, the commercial editions of CFEngine support the following types of promises in agent bundles:
>
> - databases: to manipulate and configure databases
> - environments: to manipulate and configure virtual environments
> - outputs: to more conveniently configure the logging levels of different bundles
> - services: to configure Windows system services

common
> Bundles of this type are just like agent bundles, but are special in that the variables and classes defined in them are automatically available to every other bundle in your policy. As such, they are a good place to define globally useful variables and classes. For example:

```
bundle common g
{
  vars:
      "localdir"    string => "/usr/local";
      "confdir"     string => "/etc";
  classes:
      "testhost"    or => { "testhost1", "testhost2" };
}
```

This example defines two variables with strings that will be useful in other parts of the policy, and which we can reference as $(g.localdir) and $(g.confdir) (in general, any variable can be accessed from anywhere else by prefixing it with the name of the bundle where it was defined). Also defined is a class based on whether either of the classes testhost1 or testhost2 is defined (this would be the case if the current host has any of those names, and is a common way of defining a class for a certain group of hosts—more on this in "Defining Classes for Groups of Hosts" on page 136). This class is automatically made global, which means it can be used in any other bundle.

Class and Variable Scoping

All variables in CFEngine are local to the bundle in which they are defined. However, they can be accessed from any other bundle by prefixing them with the bundle name in which they are defined, separated by a dot, as in $(g.localdir).

Most classes in CFEngine are local to the bundle in which they are defined, and they cannot be accessed from anywhere else (there is no mechanism for specifying the bundle of a class). The exceptions are:

- Classes defined in a common bundle are automatically global.
- Classes defined by the classes attribute in a promise (as a result of its status) are automatically global. This is useful because these classes are commonly used as a signaling mechanism across promises and bundles.

Note that common bundles are not necessarily evaluated before regular agent bundles, although this is a common misconception. You can (and should) put them in bundlesequence to ensure they are evaluated at the correct moment (normally, you would put them at the beginning of the execution sequence, to ensure the values defined in them are properly available to all other bundles).

edit_line

Bundles of type edit_line can be used to change a file, one of the most common and most complex operations performed by CFEngine. These bundles must be specified as the value of the edit_line attribute in a file-editing promise (this is, a promise of type files:). edit_line bundles themselves can be quite complex and contain their own set of allowable promise types, which include:

- `insert_lines:` to add lines to a file
- `delete_lines:` to remove lines from a file
- `field_edits:` to make field-oriented changes in a file
- `replace_patterns:` to make regular expression substitutions in a file

server

Bundles of type `server` control the behavior of the *cf-serverd* process, which has the task of serving files to other CFEngine machines that request them (*cf-serverd* normally runs on the CFEngine policy hub). This type of bundle can contain two promise types:

- `access:` to define access permissions to different resources on the server.
- `roles:` to define which users can indicate classes (and which classes they can define) in the server process, to alter the behavior of the `cf-serverd` daemon. One of CFEngine's strong security features is that remote machines can never execute arbitrary commands. Instead, they can execute certain bundles. Some users, as defined by `roles:` promises, may have the ability to set custom classes when invoking those remote promises, thus allowing them to modify the promises' behavior, but only as allowed by the remote bundle and its handling of the defined classes.

knowledge

Bundles of type `knowledge` are fully supported only in commercial editions of CFEngine, and allow you to document high-level system knowledge in the CFEngine configuration. This can be used to analyze the system, and to both keep and deduce information about its behavior and its configuration.

- `inferences:` specifies relationships between different concepts in the knowledge base, and performs some simple contextual reasoning
- `things:` specifies tangible objects in the knowledge map, and how they are called, how they behave, how they are connected to others, and other properties (for example, who does a machine belong to, and where it is located)
- `topics:` defines the elements (subjects and objects) that will be used in the knowledge representations, and the relationships between them
- `occurrences:` defines documents or resources (e.g., URLs) that refer to certain topics, and provides more information about them

Knowledge bundles can be analyzed by the *cf-know* command to produce and analyze knowledge maps. CFEngine's knowledge-management features are an advanced topic that we will not discuss further in this book.

monitor

Bundles of this type are supported only in commercial editions of CFEngine. They define custom parameters that CFEngine can monitor automatically, and specify how to react to changes in their values. CFEngine natively knows how to monitor a large set of system values, such as CPU and memory utilization. This type of bundle supports only one section called `measurements:`, which contains promises defining what and how to monitor it, and how to react to changes.

Certain generic promise types are allowed in all bundle types:

- `vars:` to define variables
- `classes:` to define classes
- `reports:` to define produced output

Bodies

Bodies, also called *compound bodies*, are collections of attributes and values that can be used as values to other attributes. Bodies cannot contain promises nor sections, although they can receive arguments, and can contain class expressions to specify different values for some of the attributes. Bodies, just like bundles, have a type, which indicates the attribute to which they can be passed, as well as the attributes they can contain. The generic structure of a compound body is:

```
body type name(arguments)
{
  attribute1 => value1;
  attribute2 => value2;
  …
[class_expression::]
  attributeN => valueN;
}
```

Some common compound bodies you will use include:

- `control` bodies are special containers that are not referenced in any promises, but that control the behavior of different aspects of CFEngine itself. There are different types of control bodies, depending on the component whose behavior they control. The one you are bound to use is the `common control` body. Among other things, it is in this body that you specify which bundles will be executed in your policy and in which order, using the `bundlesequence` attribute, and which additional files to read, using the `inputs` attribute:

    ```
    body common control
    {
            inputs => { "cfengine_stdlib.cf" };
            bundlesequence => { "test" };
    }
    ```

    This block tells CFEngine to load the file *cfengine_stdlib.cf* (this is the CFEngine standard library, as described in "CFEngine Standard Library" on page 66), and to execute the `test` bundle. Every CFEngine policy needs to have a `bundlesequence` definition, and this is most commonly done through a `common control` body. (You can also specify it with the -b option to *cf-agent*, but I normally do this only when testing policy components.)

As you might imagine, common control supports many other attributes that specify global CFEngine behavior. There are also control bodies for specific CFEngine components, including the following:

— agent control bodies to specify promise-evaluation behavior such as minimum time between consecutive evaluations of the same promise (ifelapsed), classes that tell CFEngine to abort (abortclasses), and many others.

— server control bodies to specify server behavior, such as addresses and users from which connections will be allowed (allowconnects, allowusers) and the interface to which the *cf-serverd* process should bind (bindtointerface).

— Others such as monitor control, runagent control, executor control, knowledge control, reporter control, and hub control.

- classes compound bodies specify which classes will be defined depending on the outcome of a promise. These bodies are valid attributes for all promise types. For example, consider the following file promise:

```
"/var/run/somefile"
  create => "true",
  classes => passfail;
```

In this case, passfail is the name of a compound body, of type classes, that needs to be defined somewhere else. For example:

```
body classes passfail
{
  promise_kept     => { "fileexisted" };
  promise_repaired => { "filecreated" };
  repair_failed    => { "fileerror" };
}
```

There are several things you should notice here. First, the type of the body part is classes, which means it can be used only as the value of a classes attribute in a promise. The name passfail is an arbitrary identifier. The documentation for the classes body type (*http://cf-learn.info/ref/classes-in-**) lists the attributes it can contain. In this case, if */var/run/somefile* already existed (the promise was *kept*), the fileexisted class will be defined after the promise runs. If */var/run/somefile* did not exist and CFEngine was able to create it (the promise was *repaired*), filecreated will be defined. And if the file cannot be created for some reason (the *repair failed*), the fileerror class will be defined. These classes can be used later on to control other promises. And more importantly, the passfail body can be used in many different promises, allowing for encapsulation and code reutilization.

An important thing to notice is that body parts can also have parameters, which allows even further customization of their behavior. For example, suppose we want the repaired/kept/failed classes to contain an arbitrary identifier to help us differentiate among multiple file checks. We could define passfail as follows:

```
body classes passfail(id)
{
```

```
    promise_kept    => { "$(id)_existed" };
    promise_repaired => { "$(id)_created" };
    repair_failed   => { "$(id)_error" };
}
```

We would then have to modify the files promises to something like this:

```
"/var/run/somefile"
  create => "true",
  classes => passfail("somefile");
```

Now "somefile" is being passed as an argument to the passfail body part, and used as part of the class names to define. This means that depending on the result of the promise, the classes somefile_existed, somefile_created or somefile_error will be defined, instead of the generic names we had used before.

- action is another attribute that can be used in any promise, and defines how the promise should be evaluated and fixed. Using it we can define that promises should only be checked but not fixed, whether the actions related to the promise should occur in the background, how often promises should be checked, logging behavior for the promise, and other attributes. For example, the following promise will warn if a certain line does not exist in /etc/motd, and will issue the warning only every hour, even if CFEngine checks more frequently:

```
bundle agent test
{
  files:
      "/etc/motd"
        edit_lines => insert_lines("Unauthorized access will be prosecuted."),
        action => warn_hourly;
}

body action warn_hourly
{
        action_policy => "warn"; # Produce warning only, don't fix anything
        ifelapsed => "60";
}
```

- copy_from is an attribute that can be used only in files: promises, and indicates from where and how a file will be copied. It is an extremely flexible attribute, since it allows us to request local or remote file copies, how the files will be compared, whether the file will be encrypted in transit, and many other parameters. For example, the following two bodies are from CFEngine's standard library:

```
body copy_from secure_cp(from,server)
{
        source    => "$(from)";
        servers   => { "$(server)" };
        compare   => "digest";
        encrypt   => "true";
        verify    => "true";
}

body copy_from remote_cp(from,server)
```

```
{
        servers    => { "$(server)" };
        source     => "$(from)";
        compare    => "mtime";
}
```

Both handle copying files from a remote server, and take both a server address and a source file as arguments. The first one specifies that the connection will be encrypted (using an internal CFEngine mechanism), that the files will be verified after copying them, and that files will be compared by computing a cryptographic hash of their contents. The second one is simpler, indicating no need for encryption or verification, and the comparison will be made using simply the time of last modification (mtime) of both files. The former, more expensive verification mechanism allows us to reliably detect changes in the files in cases when their modification date might not be a reliable indicator. In both cases, the comparison mechanism allows CFEngine to skip the expensive copy operation if the files already match.

- depth_search is another attribute of files: promises that allows us to control recursive operations. It specifies how deep to traverse, which directories to skip, and other parameters. For example:

```
body depth_search recurse_ignore(d,list)
{
        depth => "$(d)";
        exclude_dirs => { @(list) };
}
```

This definition specifies that only directories up to $(d) levels deep will be traversed (the special string "inf" can be used to specify infinite recursion), and allows the caller to specify a list of directories to exclude.

Putting copy_from and depth_search together, we can already create a functional file-copy promise:

```
bundle agent update_inputs
{
  vars:
      "server"  string => "10.1.1.1";
      "inputs"  string => "/var/cfengine/masterfiles/inputs";
  files:
      "$(sys.workdir)/inputs"
        copy_from => remote_cp("$(server)", "$(inputs)"),
        depth_search => recurse_ignore("inf", { "_.*" });
}
```

Here we will be copying all files from the directory /var/cfengine/masterfiles/inputs on server 10.1.1.1 onto the local /var/cfengine/inputs directory ($(sys.workdir) is an internal variable that CFEngine defines to be its working directory, normally /var/cfengine). A recursive copy of infinite depth will be done, but all directories starting with _ will be ignored (the patterns provided have to be regular expressions and not shell metacharacter expressions, hence the _.* instead of just _*). Note that it is not possible to use depth_search in conjunction with edit_line. For editing files, the precise file to be edited needs to be specified.

- edit_defaults is an attribute of files: promises that controls parameters of the file-editing process. You can specify whether backups should be made of the original file, the maximum size of a reasonable file for editing, and whether the file should be emptied and recreated every time. In the following example, timestamped copies of the file will be kept every time the file is changed:

```
bundle agent editexample
{
  files:
      "/etc/motd"
        create => "true",
        edit_line => insert_lines("Unauthorized use will be prosecuted"),
        edit_defaults => backup_timestamp;
}

body edit_defaults backup_timestamp
{
        empty_file_before_editing => "false";
        edit_backup => "timestamp";
        max_file_size => "300000";
}
```

- edit_field is an attribute of field_edits: promises that performs field-based editing in a file (it must be specified as an attribute in a promise of type field_edits:, which in turn is allowable only inside edit_line bundles). It specifies what characters to use as delimiters and which actions will be taken on which fields. For example, the following definition from *cfengine_stdlib.cf* performs generic field-editing operations using user-provided information:

```
body edit_field col(split,col,newval,method)
{
        field_separator    => "$(split)";
        select_field       => "$(col)";
        value_separator    => ",";
        field_value        => "$(newval)";
        field_operation    => "$(method)";
        extend_fields      => "true";
        allow_blank_fields => "true";
}
```

The split argument specifies a regular expression to use as separator (thus it gets assigned to the field_separator attribute), col indicates the column on which to operate and gets assigned to select_field (by default CFEngine starts counting from one, although this behavior can be changed using the start_fields_from_zero attribute in the edit_field body), newval indicates the value to insert or delete from that field (it gets used for field_value, each field can contain multiple values separated by value_separator, a comma in this case), and method indicates which operation to perform (set, delete, append, prepend, etc.).

The col() body definition is used in *cfengine_stdlib.cf*, for example, to edit colon-separated files, such as */etc/passwd* in Unix systems:

```
bundle edit_line set_user_field(user,field,val)

# Set the value of field number "field" in
# a :-field formatted file like /etc/passwd

{
  field_edits:

    "$(user):.*"

      comment => "Edit a user attribute in the password file",
      edit_field => col(":","$(field)","$(val)","set");
}
```

This bundle takes three arguments: the user to edit ($(user)), the field number to edit ($(field)), and the value to set in that field ($(val)). In field_edits: promises, the promiser is interpreted as a regular expression that is matched against all the lines in the file, to select which lines to edit. In this case, the value of the $(user) parameter is used to select the line that starts with that string, followed by a colon and any other text ("$(user):.*" —the pattern is automatically anchored by CFEngine to the beginning and end of the line, so there is no need for the ^ character to specify that the pattern must start at the beginning of the line). Once a line is selected, the edit_field attribute uses col() to perform the actual field-change operation, The separator is specified as a colon, the field number and the new value are passed directly from the arguments $(field) and $(val), and the operation to perform is "set", which tells CFEngine to replace the old value of the field with the new one.

To put this in context, note that set_user_field() is an edit_line bundle, which means it has to be used as the argument to the edit_line attribute of a files: promise. For example:

```
files:
  # Set the 7th field (shell) of user "nobody" to "/bin/false"
  "/etc/passwd"
    edit_line => set_user_field("nobody", "7", "/bin/false");
```

Many other compound-body attributes are allowed in CFEngine for different promise types. I have shown here some of the most common ones, but you can find the full listing and details in the CFEngine reference manual (*http://cf-learn.info/ref/*).

Bundles and Bodies Summary

The distinction between bundles and bodies can be confusing at first. Remembering these points may help:

- Bodies are named groups of *attributes*, whereas bundles are collections of *promises*. Promises are the units that actually *do something* in CFEngine (for example, run a command or add a line to a file), whereas attributes specify characteristics of how things are done (for example, whether to run the command in a shell, or where in the file to add the line).

- The value of an attribute can be a basic data type (string, integer, list, etc.), it can be the name of a body, or it can be the name of a bundle.

- The type of an attribute's value is fixed, and determined by the attribute itself (for example, the value of the `depth_search` attribute in a `files:` promise is always a body, and the value of an `edit_line` attribute is always a bundle).

- For bodies and bundles, their type is always the name of the attribute to which they correspond. For example, bodies to be used with the `depth_search` attribute are always declared as "`body depth_search xyz`", where `xyz` is an arbitrary name of your choosing. The same goes for bundles: bundles to be used with the `edit_line` attribute are always declared as "`bundle edit_line xyz`".

  There are only four types of "top level" bundles that are not used as arguments to attributes: `agent`, `server`, `knowledge` and `monitor`.

- The promise types (sections) that can appear in a bundle are determined by the bundle type. For example, `commands:` promises can only appear in bundles of type `agent`.

Normal Ordering

CFEngine does not have any flow control statements, at least not in the sense with which you may be familiar from imperative programming languages (the concept of implicit flow control may be familiar to you if you have done any declarative programming before, for example in Prolog). A lot of the behavior of CFEngine is hard-coded, and this includes the order in which things are evaluated. This is called *normal ordering*, and is determined based on what makes sense for different types of bundles and promises. For example, it makes no sense to first create a file and then delete it, while it makes sense to first delete it and then create it again. Normal ordering can, if needed, be overriden by defining classes after an operation completes, and then defining other operations based on that class (for details, see "Controlling Promise Execution Order" on page 138).

Bundles of type `common` are a good place to define variables and classes that will be accessible to all other bundles in the policy. All classes in common bundles are global, and all variables in them are accessible from other bundles by prefixing them with the bundle name, as in `$(bundle.variable)`.

CFEngine has mechanisms to detect variable/class dependencies and a best-effort algorithm to make sure all necessary values are available before an expression or promise is evaluated. You can help it ensure consistency and convergence by including bundles of type common in the bundlesequence declaration, even though this is not strictly needed.

For agent bundles, CFEngine will execute them up to three times in an attempt to achieve a convergent state. In each iteration, the sections in the bundle will be executed in the following order (sections marked with * are only available in commercial editions of CFEngine):

1. vars
2. classes
3. outputs *
4. interfaces
5. files

   In turn, within edit_line bundles, the following order will be kept:

   a. vars
   b. classes
   c. delete_lines
   d. field_edits
   e. insert_lines
   f. replace_patterns
   g. reports

6. packages
7. environments *
8. methods
9. processes
10. services
11. commands
12. storage
13. databases *
14. reports

Within each section, promises will be executed in the order in which they appear in the policy. Multiple executions of each bundle mean that you can, for example, define a variable, then define a class based on that variable, and then define other variables depending on that class. The three iterations may not be executed in all cases - if there are no promises repaired during an iteration, then CFEngine assumes the bundle has converged, and stops further iterations.

Within server bundles, the normal ordering is as follows:

1. vars
2. classes
3. access
4. roles

Within monitor bundles, the normal ordering is as follows:

1. vars
2. classes
3. measurements *
4. reports

Finally, within knowledge bundles, the normal ordering is as follows:

1. vars
2. classes
3. topics
4. occurrences
5. inferences
6. reports

Normal ordering provides a fairly rigid structure to the execution of CFEngine policies. It is common when you first start writing CFEngine policies, particularly if you are familiar with imperative programming, to try to "fight" the normal ordering to fit what you want to do. When you encounter a case in which you are positive that normal ordering needs to be changed, I encourage you to back up and rethink at a higher level the task you want to accomplish. Most of the time, you will find that structuring the task in some other way will make the need to reorder operations go away, and will in fact make more sense with the way CFEngine "thinks."

Looping in CFEngine

One of the most evident examples of "thinking in CFEngine" is the concept of *implicit looping*. It is one of the most basic behaviors, one of the most confusing to a CFEngine beginner, and one of the most powerful once you harness it.

First, let us define it: in CFEngine 3, if you refer to a list variable (normally called @(var)) as a scalar ($(var)), CFEngine interprets it to mean "iterate over all the values in the list."

Let's try it. Type in the following policy:

```
body common control
{
        bundlesequence => { "test" };
}

bundle agent test
{
  vars:
      "colors" slist => { "red", "green", "blue" };
  reports:
    cfengine::
      "$(colors)";
}
```

Now run it:

```
$ cf-agent -KI -f ./looping1.cf
R: red
R: green
R: blue
```

The lines that start with "R: " indicate messages produced by the reports: promises in the policy. You can see that the single promise in the reports: section has been repeated for every value in the list, therefore printing all the values.

You can also try nested looping:

```
bundle agent test
{
  vars:
      "colors" slist => { "red", "green", "blue" };
      "tone"   slist => { "dark", "light" };
  reports:
    cfengine_3::
      "$(tone) $(colors)";
}
```

This returns the following:

```
$ cf-agent -K -f ./looping2.cf
R: dark red
R: light red
R: dark green
R: light green
R: dark blue
R: light blue
```

Simple enough, isn't it? In this explicit example, the behavior is clear. The real power of implicit looping comes when you realize that it can be used in *any* type of promise, and that it means the *whole promise* will be executed as many times as there are items in the list. Also, the looping variable can be used anywhere—in defining variables or classes, in executing commands, or in making decisions with classes.

Let's look at a real example in which implicit looping saved the day (this was, inciden-
tally, the time when this really "clicked" in my head as I was starting with CFEngine
3). I needed to determine which network interface in a system was configured in a
certain network segment, to apply some configuration commands.

CFEngine has a built-in array variable called sys.ipv4 that contains the IP addresses of
all the network interfaces in the system, indexed by interface name. My first thought
was that I needed a function that gave me all the values stored in this array, so I could
compare them against my desired IP address range and find the one I needed.

To my surprise, I realized that CFEngine has a getindices() function, but no equivalent
getvalues() function (actually this function was added as of version 3.1.5, but wasn't
available when I came up with this solution, and in any case this is much more elegant).
After turning the problem over a lot in my head, I came to the realization that the
getvalues() function is not needed in this case. Here is the code I came up with:

```
body common control
{
        bundlesequence => { "find_netif" };
}

bundle agent find_netif
{
  vars:
      "nics" slist => getindices("sys.ipv4"); ❶
      # Regex we want to match on the IP address
      "ipregex" string => "192\.168\.1\..*";

  classes:
      "ismatch_$(nics)" expression => regcmp("$(ipregex)", "$(sys.ipv4[$(nics)])"); ❷

  reports:
    cfengine::
      "NICs found: $(nics) ($(sys.ipv4[$(nics)]))"; ❸

      "Matched NIC: $(nics) ($(sys.ipv4[$(nics)]))"
        ifvarclass => "ismatch_$(nics)";
}
```

Let us look at this in detail.

❶ First, we get a list (using getindices()) of all the network interfaces in the system,
and store it in the nics variable. We also assign into ipregex the regular expression
for the IP address range I want to match (in this case, 192.168.1.*).

❷ Then we use this list, referenced as a scalar, in the classes: promise, to define a
number of classes named after each of the interfaces, by using $(nics) in the class
name itself. The definition of the class depends on whether the IP address of that
network interface ($(nics) is used again in the call to the regcmp() method) matches
the regular expression of the IP address I want to find. The result is that, for each

NIC on the system, the corresponding class is defined if its IP address matches, and undefined if it does not.

❸ Finally, we print all the interfaces by using $(nics) in a report message, and we also print only the matching ones by conditioning the second message using the ifvarclass => "ismatch_$(nics)" attribute. The reference to $(nics) in the ifvar class attribute is also expanded to each value in turn, so the second message is printed only for those NICs whose corresponding class is defined.

So you see, we do not need the getvalues() function after all. In this example I used the defined classes to print messages, but in my real example I used them to append the appropriate configuration statements to a file—but only for those interfaces that matched the IP range I wanted.

I encourage you to look at that example again, and make sure you understand it. There are no looping constructs anywhere—in fact, they do not exist in the CFEngine syntax at all. It may take a while getting used to this. Whenever you are constructing a policy and you think "I definitely need a while loop to do this," take a step back and see whether you can recast the problem using implicit looping. The definition of classes based on a condition using implicit looping is a powerful technique, and you will see it used in many of the examples in this book.

Thinking in CFEngine

As we have seen, CFEngine imposes a rigid structure on many aspects of its operation. Two prime examples are normal ordering and implicit looping, which help get rid of the need for explicit control flow statements. For the most part, you do not tell CFEngine how to do things. Rather, you tell it *what you want to achieve* and write out the low-level building blocks of how to achieve certain promises, and CFEngine will put them together for you to bring the system to the desired state.

If you are like me, you have been programming for some time before you encountered CFEngine, and your brain is wired to think about problems and tasks in a certain way. This will almost inevitably cause a clash when you have to "let go" of the control and lend it over to CFEngine.

I have personally found that what works for me is to "step back" from the details of the task at hand, and think at a higher level: "what am I trying to achieve?" Often this gives a different perspective on why you are doing certain things, and how you are trying to achieve them. My main advice is to keep practicing, and to use the community resources available to study examples and to get feedback on your promises from more experienced users.

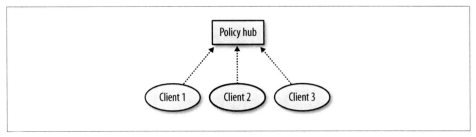

Figure 3-2. The simplest form of CFEngine distributed deployment, with a single policy hub and multiple clients

Clients and Servers

One of CFEngine's key strengths is autonomy. A machine in which CFEngine is installed and configured does not need a network connection to operate, and as long as its policies are well defined, it will continue to obey those policies and maintain the system as configured. For instance, a laptop that is sometimes connected to the company network, but is also often away, will continue to benefit from CFEngine running on it.

However, the true power of CFEngine lies in its ability to manage thousands of machines with very little effort, and for this you need to distribute the corresponding policies to all those hosts. Fortunately, CFEngine makes it very easy to set up a client-server environment in which one or more hosts act as policy hubs, distributing policies and data to others. As we saw in "Finishing the Installation and Bootstrapping" on page 16, all it requires is a single command to configure CFEngine and tell it which machine to use as its policy hub:

```
cf-agent --bootstrap --policy-server x.y.z.w
```

This command works on both the policy hub itself and its clients. In the hub, *cf-agent* will recognize its own IP address and configure the host as a policy hub.

In its simplest form, and one perfectly suitable for all but the largest of organizations, you can have a single policy hub with multiple clients fetching policies and files from it, as shown in Figure 3-2.

In larger and more complex environments, you can have a more complex structure. A CFEngine policy hub can itself be a client for some other hub, thus creating a hierarchy of CFEngine policy distribution points, as shown in Figure 3-3.

The need for a hierarchical structure could be dictated by technical requirements (e.g., geographically disperse sites, low-bandwidth links between them, traffic blocking) or administrative needs (e.g., different teams in charge of different locations, needing to make their own customizations to the top-level inherited policies). CFEngine is flexible enough to accomodate any of them. Ideally, all the policy files should propagate from the top-level, where they are maintained in a master repository, but you could also have several disjoint trees in your organization.

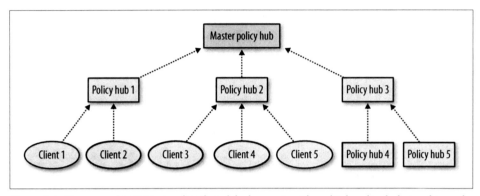

Figure 3-3. More complex CFEngine distributed deployment, with multiple policy hubs in a hierarchy

CFEngine follows a strict pull-only philosophy: only the client can make requests to the server, asking for the information and files it needs. The server cannot push anything onto the clients. This convention makes it very simple to configure the network to allow communication between CFEngine clients and servers. Only one port—TCP/5308— is necessary for the client to connect to the server. All communication, including file transfers, takes place through this port.

> The *cf-runagent* command can be used on the server to contact the clients. In this case port, TCP/5308 also needs to be open from the server to the clients, and *cf-serverd* needs to be running on the clients to process those connections. Note, however, that *cf-runagent* does not allow the server to execute arbitrary commands on the clients. All that it does is instruct *cf-agent* on the client to "wake up" and process its policies immediately, instead of waiting for the next scheduled run. We will see the details of this configuration in "CFEngine Remote Execution Using cf-runagent" on page 63.

The decision to only allow the clients to pull from the server (and not the server to push things onto the clients) is also rooted in promise theory. An entity cannot make promises about anyone other than itself. Because of this, the operation of a distributed system cannot depend on one entity forcing others to do something. Entities may request information from others, but they may make promises only about their own behavior. *Voluntary cooperation* is one of CFEngine's core principles.

On the other hand, CFEngine is designed with resilience and graceful degradation in mind. If a client becomes disconnected from the network, CFEngine continues managing it using the latest locally-stored version of the policies until it restores connectivity. This allows clients to continue working during network outages, network congestion, security incidents, or other circumstances that may prevent connectivity to the master policy hub.

CFEngine Server Configuration

The CFEngine server functionality is provided by the *cf-serverd* process. It is configured using a `server control` body block like in the following example, taken from the default configuration provided with CFEngine (this is part of the */var/cfengine/inputs/promises.cf* file generated when you bootstrap CFEngine):

```
body server control
{
        denybadclocks        => "false";
        allowconnects        => { "127.0.0.1" , "::1", @(def.acl) };
        allowallconnects     => { "127.0.0.1" , "::1", @(def.acl) };
        trustkeysfrom        => { "127.0.0.1" , "::1", @(def.acl) };

        skipverify           => { ".*$(def.domain)", "127.0.0.1" , "::1", @(def.acl) };

        allowusers           => { "root" };
        maxconnections       => "100";

        # Uncomment the line below to allow remote users to run
        # cf-agent through cf-runagent

        # cfruncommand        => "$(sys.cf_agent)";
}
```

 The default policy files produced by CFEngine when you bootstrap a client are an excellent starting point and provide a lot of basic functionality, but it is highly recommended you go over them and customize them to your particular needs and infrastructure.

This body defines the set of machines from which connections will be allowed (`allowconnects`), those that will be allowed to connect multiple times simultaneously (`allowallconnects`),[1] those whose public keys will be trusted if they have not been seen before (`trustkeysfrom`) and those whose DNS record will not be checked for consistency (`skipverify`). Also specified are the maximum number of simultaneous connections (`maxconnections`), the users that will be allowed to connect (`allowusers`), and whether machines with out-of-sync clocks will be blocked (`denybadclocks`).

Additionally, per-directory and per-file ACLs can be defined in the `access_rules()` bundle, whose default version contains the following:

```
bundle server access_rules()
{
  access:
    any::
      "$(def.dir_masterfiles)"
        handle => "server_access_rule_grant_access_policy",
        comment => "Grant access to the policy updates",
```

---

1. Normally each host is allowed only one connection at a time

```
            admit => { ".*$(def.domain)", @(def.acl) };
        roles:
    }
```

This bundle contains promises of type access:, which define the ACLs to apply. In this case, directory $(def.dir_masterfiles) (which expands by default to /var/cfengine/masterfiles) will be accessible by all machines in the $(def.domain) domain, plus those defined explicitly in the @(def.acl) list.

Note that most of these parameters include the @(def.acl) and $(def.domain) variables. These are references to the acl and domain variables defined in the def() bundle, which is included in the same file:

```
bundle common def
{
  vars:
      "domain"  string => "example.com",  ❶
        comment => "Define a global domain for all hosts",
        handle => "common_def_vars_domain";
      "acl" slist => {
                        "$(sys.policy_hub)/16"  ❷
                     },
        comment => "Define an acl for the machines to be granted accesses",
        handle => "common_def_vars_acl";
      "dir_masterfiles" string => translatepath("$(sys.workdir)/masterfiles"),
        comment => "Define masterfiles path",
        handle => "common_def_vars_dir_masterfiles";
}
```

You are expected to edit the def() bundle before putting CFEngine into production, in particular two values:

❶ The $(domain) variable must contain the domain name of your current environment. This is used in the code shown earlier to limit access to machines from this domain. It is also used in some other contexts in the default *promises.cf* file.

❷ The @(acl) variable is a list containing all the IP addresses that should have access to the server. This promise uses the value of $(sys.policy_hub) (an automatically-set variable that contains the IP address of the hub from which the host was bootstrapped) and determines its local class-B network (/16). The assumption is that the policy hub will in most cases be in the same network as the client. Of course, this range may well be too broad or too narrow according to your needs, so you must edit it accordingly.

Updating Client Files from the Server

One of the main tasks of the policy hub is to distribute policy files, and any other necessary files, to its clients. This is a crucial operation, since it makes it possible to update files on the hub and have them propagate automatically to all the clients. To this effect, CFEngine provides ample capabilities for efficient and secure file transfer.

The default policy installed with CFEngine contains a bundle called `update()` which is executed *on the clients* (remember that the CFEngine policy hub cannot instruct the clients to do anything). It takes care of all these tasks automatically, but you may want to modify it according to your needs. It is contained in the file */var/cfengine/inputs/failsafe.cf*, and in a nutshell these are the tasks it performs:

- Check whether the host key files exist (under */var/cfengine/ppkeys/*), and run *cf-key* to create them if they are not present.
- Start the *cf-serverd*, *cf-monitord* and *cf-execd* processes if they are not running.
- Copy updated files from */var/cfengine/masterfiles/* on the policy hub to */var/cfengine/inputs/* on all machines (both the clients and the policy hub) to put them in production.
- Copy updated CFEngine binaries from */var/cfengine/bin/* to */usr/local/sbin/*.
- Ensure all critical directories and files have the correct permissions.

For now we will look only at the file-copying operations, but I encourage you to read through the whole bundle to get an idea of what it does. These are the crucial parts:

```
bundle agent update
{
  vars:
      "inputs_dir" string => translatepath("$(sys.workdir)/inputs"),   ❶
        comment => "Directory containing Cfengine policies",
        handle => "update_vars_inputs_dir";
      "master_location" string => "/var/cfengine/masterfiles",   ❷
        comment => "The master cfengine policy directory on the policy host",
        handle => "update_vars_master_location";
  files:
      "$(inputs_dir)"   ❸
        comment => "Copy policy updates from master source on policy server",
        handle => "update_files_inputs_dir",
        copy_from => u_rcp("$(master_location)","$(sys.policy_hub)"),   ❹
        depth_search => u_recurse("inf"),   ❺
        file_select  => u_input_files,   ❻
        classes => u_if_repaired("update_report");   ❼
}
```

❶ The `$(inputs_dir)` variable contains the directory where the local CFEngine installation expects to find its policy files. On Unix/Linux hosts this is normally */var/cfengine/inputs*, but the location can vary in different platforms. For this reason, we are using the `$(sys.workdir)` variable, which is automatically defined to be the base directory of the local CFEngine installation. We are also using the `translatepath()` function to translate the Unix-style path into the local style (for example, using backslashes instead of forward slashes on Windows).

❷ The `$(master_location)` variable contains the directory on the policy hub where the "master files" are located, and from where they will be copied to the local host. The policy hub has to be a Unix-style host, so in this case we don't need to perform any path translation.

❸ The `files:` promise is the one that does the actual work. The promiser is the destination directory `$(inputs_dir)`, to which the files will be copied according to the parameters specified by the promise attributes that follow.

❹ The `copy_from` attribute indicates the source of the files. The value of this attribute is a compound body, defined in the same *failsafe.cf* file as follows:

```
body copy_from u_rcp(from,server)
{
        source      => "$(from)";
        compare     => "digest";
        trustkey    => "true";
    !am_policy_hub::
        servers => { "$(server)" };
}
```

This body receives as arguments the directory and the host from where the files should be copied. `$(master_location)` is the variable defined before, and `$(sys.policy_hub)` is a special CFEngine variable that is set when the client is bootstrapped, as described in "Finishing the Installation and Bootstrapping" on page 16. Additionally, it indicates that the files should be compared using a cryptographic digest (`compare => "digest"`), and that the client should trust the cryptographic keys presented by the server (`trustkey => "true"`). The `servers` attribute is set only when the `am_policy_hub` class is not set, and `am_policy_hub` is a hard class set only on the policy hub, so the effect is that on the policy hub, the file copy operation will be done locally, from */var/cfengine/masterfiles/* to */var/cfengine/inputs/*.

❺ The `depth_search` attribute is used to indicate a recursive file copy operation of infinite depth. Its value is another compound body:

```
body depth_search u_recurse(d)
{
        depth => "$(d)";
        exclude_dirs => { "\.svn" };
}
```

The `depth` attribute is set to the passed argument (which can be a number, or the special value `"inf"` for infinite recursion). The `exclude_dirs` attribute is also used to skip version-control directories that may be present in the server (assuming that version control is done using Subversion).

❻ The `file_select` attribute is used to control which types of files are copied. This is another compound body:

```
body file_select u_input_files
{
        leaf_name => { ".*.cf",".*.dat",".*.txt" };
        file_result => "leaf_name";
}
```

In this case we are asking CFEngine to copy only files whose names end with .cf, .dat and .txt. There are many criteria that can be specified in a file_select body, and for this reason we need the file_result attribute to tell CFEngine on which criteria we want to match (in this case it is the only one available).

❼ The classes attribute indicates that if any files are copied (which flags the promise as "repaired"), then the update_report class should be set. This class can be used in other parts of the policy to execute any actions necessary (for example, produce a report) when the files are updated. This is yet another compound body that sets the appropriate class:

```
body classes u_if_repaired(x)
{
        promise_repaired => { "$(x)" };
}
```

File-copy promises are extremely flexible and powerful. Policy and binary updates are automatically handled by the built-in CFEngine policies, but I encourage you to read the documentation for files: promises (*http://cf-learn.info/ref/files-in-agent-promises*) to get a good idea of the wide range of tasks they can perform.

 Why is this bundle in the *failsafe.cf* file instead of the *promises.cf* file? The default CFEngine policy instructs *cf-execd* (this is defined in the body executor control in *promises.cf*) to always evaluate *failsafe.cf* before running *promises.cf*, to ensure that all files are properly updated. Additionally, if there is any failure in policy evaluation, *cf-agent* automatically tries to load *failsafe.cf*, which must be designed to be standalone and to perform any reparation tasks necessary to bring CFEngine back into operation.

CFEngine Remote Execution Using cf-runagent

One of the basic premises of CFEngine is that clients operate autonomously. If there is a central coordination point, like the policy hub, it is up to the clients to connect to it and fetch policies or files. However, in practice, the server (or some other machine) sometimes needs to "ping" the clients and ask them to do something. This is where *cf-runagent* comes in. It does not allow arbitrary actions to be executed, but simply asks the remote machine to run *cf-agent* and evaluate its policies. The remote host (in most cases it would be a CFEngine client) needs to have *cf-serverd* running and configured to listen for connections from *cf-runagent*.

Allow me to emphasize this point: *cf-runagent* does not allow the execution of arbitrary commands or arbitrary actions on a remote host. It simply instructs the host to run *cf-agent* and start evaluating its policies. This is useful when you don't want to wait until the next regular execution of *cf-agent* (for example, critical policy or operating system updates).

The behavior of the *cf-runagent* command can be configured as part of the CFEngine policy in a runagent control body, which allows you to specify, among other things, a list of hosts that will be contacted by default when running the command. On the client side (the one to which the *cf-runagent* command will connect), the server control body specifies whether *cf-runagent* connections will be allowed, and what they will be allowed to do. It can also specify a list of remote users that will be allowed to set custom classes when running *cf-runagent*. This allows more fine-grained control of the policy behavior.

cf-runagent connections are handled by *cf-serverd*, so if you need this functionality you will also need to open port TCP/5308 traffic from the server to the clients.

Because of its potential security implications, the *cf-runagent* functionality comes disabled in the CFEngine default policy. To enable it, you need to uncomment the cfruncommand attribute in the server control body, shown in "CFEngine Server Configuration" on page 59:

```
cfruncommand        => "$(sys.cf_agent)";
```

This instructs *cf-serverd* to listen for connections from *cf-runagent*, and to execute *cf-agent* in response to them (remember that this is all that *cf-runagent* allows you to do: wake up *cf-agent*). We still need to instruct cf-serverd to allow access to the *cf-agent* binary (its path is stored in the special variable $(sys.cf_agent), normally */var/cfengine/bin/cf-agent*) from the policy hub. We need to do this in the access_rules() bundle:

```
bundle server access_rules()
{
 access:
  any::
...
   "$(sys.cf_agent)"
     handle => "grant_access_policy_agent",
     comment => "Grant access to the agent (for cf-runagent)",
     admit => { "$(sys.policy_hub)" };
}
```

In this case, we are telling *cf-serverd* to allow access to the *cf-agent* binary only to the policy hub, as defined by the special variable $(sys.policy_hub).

Finally, we need to tell the policy hub which hosts to contact by default when *cf-runagent* is executed. We need to do this explicitly in the runagent control body:

```
body runagent control
{
    # A list of hosts to contact when using cf-runagent

  any::

    hosts => { "127.0.0.1" };

  # , "myhost.example.com:5308", ...

}
```

Note that defining this list is not strictly necessary, as the list of hosts can be specified in the command line when running *cf-runagent*, using the `--hail` option.

CFEngine Information Resources

CFEngine has been around for a long time, and it has developed a solid body of documentation and information. In addition to community support, the company that was formed to provide commercial support for CFEngine, CFEngine AS, provides extensive documentation and information, most of it free of charge.

One word of caution: CFEngine 3, the version we are covering in this book, was released relatively recently (January 2009), and much of the documentation found online from third parties is still geared towards CFEngine 2. While you can apply many of the basic ideas, be aware that the syntax of CFEngine 3 is completely different and incompatible with the previous version.

Let's look at some of the information resources available for CFEngine 3.

Manuals and Official Guides

Most of the documentation made available by CFEngine AS can be found at the CFEngine Manuals web page (*https://cfengine.com/manuals*). The core documentation includes the following:

- *Reference manual* (*http://cfengine.com/manuals/cf3-reference*): the most complete and authoritative reference for CFEngine concepts, installation, syntax, and examples. Be aware that the version found online is always automatically generated from the latest version of the code, so every once in a while you may find documented features that do not work on the latest official release of the code (you would need to compile the latest code from the source code repository).

- *Tutorial* (*http://cfengine.com/manuals/cf3-tutorial*): an easier-to-digest tutorial that walks you through the basic concepts and examples of installation and basic usage. Also available in the form of a *concept guide* (*http://cfengine.com/manuals/cf3-conceptguide*) that contains only the basic concepts, without the tutorial part.

- *Syntax chart* (*https://cfengine.com/syntax*): A concise chart detailing all the possible values for every command and parameter in CFEngine.

In this web page you will find documents organized by topics and by learning paths. Apart from the core documents, you will find here a growing collection of Special Topics Guides (*http://cfengine.com/special_topics*), a series of shorter documents that focus on specific advanced aspects of working with CFEngine. You can find documentation about best practices for different topics, such as team collaboration, integrating CFEngine into change management practices or specific frameworks such as the ITIL standard, reporting capabilities, knowledge management, etc.

CFEngine Standard Library

The CFEngine Standard Library (previously known as the Community Open Promise Body Library, or COPBL) contains implementations of a large number of commonly-used promise bundles and bodies. It includes bundles for tasks such as editing configuration files, interfacing with common package managers, editing text files, and copying files. The standard library allows you to focus on the task at hand without having to worry about the details, and also serves as a fantastic source of examples, allowing you to extend or define your own bundles and bodies for CFEngine configuration. This library is constantly evolving, and users are encouraged to submit changes and additions to it.

The standard library is contained in the *cfengine_stdlib.cf* file, which is included with the CFEngine distribution, and which you can also download as part of the Policy Library and Starter Kit (*http://cfengine.com/starterkit*).

 The standard library is in constant evolution at the moment, so I encourage you to download the latest version and use it to replace the one that came with your CFEngine distribution.

To use the standard library in your own configuration, you must include it in your policy, in the common control body:

```
body common control
{
    inputs => { "cfengine_stdlib.cf" };
}
```

The standard library provides you with basic building blocks for implementing different tasks using CFEngine, but it provides no ready-made solutions for complex problems. This is the role of the CFEngine Solutions Guide.

CFEngine Solutions Guide

The Solutions Guide (*http://cfengine.com/manuals/cf3-solutions.html*) is a collection of modular bundles with examples that are more complex than the building blocks included in the standard library, often corresponding to full tasks such as user creation and maintenance, email server management, or web server configuration. Some of these examples can be used as-is, but they are more suitable as starting points on which you can base your own configurations, customized to your specific needs and situation.

CFEngine Design Center

The Design Center (*https://github.com/cfengine/design-center*) is a public repository that contains *sketches*, pre-made and reusable CFEngine components for a wide variety of tasks. This repository is in constant growth thanks to contributions from the CFEngine user community. I encourage you to browse through it. You may find many things that you can reuse as-they-are, and others that could give you ideas and starting points for your own policies.

Community Forums

The official CFEngine forums are hosted at *http://cfengine.com/forum/*, and are a fantastic resource of information and help. Both CFEngine developers and advanced users participate actively in the forums, providing a friendly and fertile ground for newcomers to ask questions and learn about CFEngine, and for experienced users to exchange information, discuss advanced aspects, and provide feedback to the developers.

CFEngine Bug Tracker

Although bugs and feature requests are often first discussed in the forums, the official mechanism for reporting them is the CFEngine bug tracker (*http://bug.cfengine.com/*).

Other Community Resources

CFEngine users have also developed and made available an incredible amount of useful resources. Here is the list of some of the most useful ones.

- Neil H. Watson's CFEngine 3 Tutorial (*http://watson-wilson.ca/2011/03/cfengine -3-tutorial.html*) was one of the first tutorials available specifically for CFEngine 3, and provides a very useful, hands-on guide to CFEngine installation and setting up an initial scheme for experimenting.

- Jessica Greer's Yale University's CFEngine 3 library (*https://github.com/jlgreer/yale _cfengine3/*) shows many real-world examples of bodies and bundles used to maintain Yale's computers with CFEngine.

- Aleksey Tsalolikhin's Guide to CFEngine 3 Body of Knowledge (*http://verticalsy sadmin.com/blog/uncategorized/guide-to-cfengine-3-body-of-knowledge*) is a great collection of links to a lot of the information available about CFEngine 3, including many of the resources already mentioned.

- Jesse Becker's CFEngineers Wiki (*http://cfengineers.org/*) is a wiki born with the intention of creating a place where information and code can be shared. As of this writing it is nascent, with little content but growing.

Recommended Reading Order

As a companion to this book, I would recommend reading the CFEngine Concept Guide (*http://cfengine.com/manuals/cf3-conceptguide*) and the CFEngine Tutorial (*http: //cfengine.com/manuals/cf3-tutorial*) from CFEngine AS, and to always have the CFEngine Reference Guide handy for the full details about the CFEngine policy language. All the examples in this book make heavy use of the standard library, and some of the more complex ones are extensions of the problems shown in the CFEngine solutions guide. I strongly recommend following and participating in the CFEngine forums, and contributing as you can to resources such as the CFEngine Design Center, the CFEngineers Wiki, or through any other venue in which you are a regular participant (forums, mailing lists, etc.).

## CHAPTER 4

Using CFEngine

We will now explore how to perform some common configuration tasks using CFEngine. Along the way we will encounter more advanced concepts and structures of the CFEngine language.

Initial System Configuration

After a system is installed, a number of routine tasks needs to be performed before declaring it ready for use. These include installation of base software packages, network configuration, file system configuration, user creation, authentication configuration, and configuration of system components. CFEngine can do all of these tasks consistently and predictably.

Throughout this section, we will incrementally build a CFEngine policy that edits a number of configuration files, starting from a single entry point. In the process I will show you some common techniques for passing and processing parameters, and several new CFEngine constructs and concepts.

Editing /etc/sysctl.conf

One of the files that commonly requires configuration in a new Linux system is */etc/ sysctl.conf*. This file contains configuration values for some kernel parameters that control different aspects of system behavior. For example, it may contain the following lines:

```
net.ipv4.tcp_syncookies = 1
net.ipv4.conf.all.accept_source_route = 0
net.ipv4.conf.all.accept_redirects = 0
net.ipv4.conf.all.rp_filter = 1
net.ipv4.conf.all.log_martians = 1
```

These particular parameters control behavior of the networking stack in the kernel (net.ipv4).

We can use CFEngine to ensure these parameters are present in the */etc/sysctl.conf* file. We will walk through an example that demonstrates this ability, but also shows the different levels at which a CFEngine policy can operate:

1. At the highest level, the policy simply says "configure the */etc/sysctl.conf* file." This part of the policy is a building block that can be added or removed to an installation at a management level without worrying about how it's implemented.

2. The next level down says "set these values in the */etc/sysctl.conf* file." This can be changed as a sysadmin decides what options need to be enabled, without thinking about the syntax of the file.

3. The next level explains the structure of the file and how the parameters should be set. It essentially extracts the implementation details, which are independent of which options you choose.

4. The lowest level explains how to perform the field edits in the file, how classes should be handled, and other implementation details.

This is the code:

```
bundle agent configfiles ❶
{
  vars:
      # Files to edit
      "files[sysctl]" string => "/etc/sysctl.conf"; ❷

      # Sysctl variables to set
      "sysctl[net.ipv4.tcp_syncookies]"                string => "1"; ❸
      "sysctl[net.ipv4.conf.all.accept_source_route]"  string => "0";
      "sysctl[net.ipv4.conf.all.accept_redirects]"     string => "0";
      "sysctl[net.ipv4.conf.all.rp_filter]"            string => "1";
      "sysctl[net.ipv4.conf.all.log_martians]"         string => "1";

  methods: ❹
      "sysctl"  usebundle => edit_sysctl,
        comment => "Configure $(files[sysctl])";
}

bundle agent edit_sysctl
{
  files: ❺
      "$(configfiles.files[sysctl])"
        handle => "edit_sysctl",
        comment => "Make sure sysctl.conf contains desired configuration settings",
        create => "true",
        edit_line => set_variable_values("configfiles.sysctl"), ❻
        classes => if_repaired("sysctl_modified"); ❼

  commands: ❽
    sysctl_modified.!no_restarts::
      "/sbin/sysctl -p"
        handle => "reload_sysctl",
        comment => "Make sure new sysctl settings are loaded";
}
```

This short CFEngine policy ensures that the appropriate lines are present in the */etc/ sysctl.conf* file to set the parameters we want. If a parameter is already there but with a different value, the policy will fix it. If a parameter does not appear in the file, the policy will add it. Let's dissect the example by parts.

❶ The `configfiles()` agent bundle is a "driver" bundle that calls others to actually perform the work (see the `methods:` section later). This allows us (as we will do in later sections) to add more tasks that are called from the same driver bundle.

❷ In `configfiles()`, we first define some variables in a `vars:` section. In it, we define an array called `files`. Remember, as we saw in "Arrays" on page 36, that arrays in CFEngine are indexed by arbitrary strings. In this case we are specifying an element indexed by the string `sysctl`, and containing the path of the file to be edited. We will refer back to this array later in the policy, and we will add more elements to it throughout the chapter, to hold the filenames of the different files to edit. To refer back to this array we will use the name `configfiles.files`, to indicate the `files` array inside the `configfiles()` bundle.

❸ We also define an array called `sysctl` (I used the same name as the element defined above in `files` just because they both refer to the same file, but I could use any name), indexed by parameter name, and containing the value to set for each parameter. This is a common technique that we will use for passing key/value pairs in CFEngine, as it allows us to succinctly define values for configuration files, users, and many other parameters. Note that we define each element of the array on its own line, each element indexed by the name of a parameter to set in */etc/sysctl.conf*, and containing as its value the value to set for that parameter. We define the elements as strings to make them generic and able to contain any type of value. To refer to this array from other bundles, we will use its full name `configfiles.sysctl`, to identify the bundle where it was defined.

❹ After setting up the variables in `configfiles()`, we include a `methods:` section, which allows us to specify multiple bundles to be called in sequence. In this example, we have only the call to `edit_sysctl()`, which does the work of editing the file. (We'll describe `edit_sysctl()` in a moment.) Each method call has an arbitrary identifier. In this case we use the identifier `"sysctl"` to identify it as part of the sequence that performs the edits on */etc/sysctl.conf*. Later in the chapter we will add calls to other bundles that perform different configuration tasks. We also specify a comment attribute to express the higher-level intention of this promise.

 Using `methods:` promises to abstract lower-level bundles is a good way of communicating higher-level intentions in CFEngine policies, without the distraction of the actual implementation details.

❺ The `edit_sysctl()` bundle is called from the `methods:` section, and contains *promises* that specify the desired state of the system. The bundle starts with a `files:` section, in which the promiser is the file to be edited. We use, as the filename, the `sysctl` element of the `configfiles.files` array. This is the `files` array defined in the `configfiles()` bundle, which gives us the value `"/etc/sysctl.conf"`. We provide `handle` and `comment` attributes, which contribute nothing to the configuration activity, but are recommended in all promises because they help you tremendously when observing log output or generating documentation using CFEngine's knowledge-management tools. The `create` attribute specifies that the file should be created if it does not exist (this may be the case immediately after installation if no custom parameters are set).

❻ Next comes the part that actually does the work, and it is surprisingly simple. The `edit_line` attribute calls the `set_variable_values()` bundle with the *name* of the array that contains the values we want to set. We do not pass the array itself but its name, and this name will be dereferenced inside `set_variable_values()` to find the actual array.

You probably realize that the `set_variable_values()` bundle is very important, since it's the one that actually performs the work of editing the file. This is not a built-in command, but rather is contained in the CFEngine Standard Library (described in Page 66) which is stored in *cfengine_stdlib.cf*. We will come back to it in a moment.

❼ The `classes` attribute tells CFEngine that if the promise is *repaired*, the `sysctl_modified` class should be set (the notion of a "class" was explained in "Classes and Decision Making" on page 37.) The `if_repaired` body part is defined in *cfengine_stdlib.cf* as well.

Wait a second. What do I mean by *repaired*? To CFEngine, a promise is repaired when *any* actions needs to be taken as a result of evaluating the promise, and those actions result in reaching the desired state of the promise. For example, if the file already had the desired configuration values, CFEngine would see no need to edit it, and it would not be marked as repaired (in this case CFEngine would consider the promise as "kept"). On the other hand, if any of the parameters were not present and the promise adds them, then the promise will be flagged as "repaired." All possible end states of a promise are described in the documentation (*http://cf-learn.info/ref/classes-in-**) for the `classes` attribute. We are free to execute this bundle as many times as we want, and CFEngine will make changes only when they are needed. Thus is the nature of convergent configuration that CFEngine allows us to perform.

❽ If the file did not contain all the configuration parameters and CFEngine adds any of them (thus "repairing" the state of the file), the `sysctl_modified` class will be set, thanks to the `if_repaired` body part we just saw in our configuration. This is useful because when the file gets modified, we have to issue the */sbin/sysctl -p* command to instruct the system to reload the values and make them effective immediately. Thus, in the `commands:` section, you can see that we are issuing this command. The command is preceded by a *class expression*:

```
sysctl_modified.!no_restarts::
```

This is a boolean expression in which the dot means AND (you can also use an ampersand if it feels more natural), and the exclamation mark means NOT. (A vertical bar or pipe character, which is not used in this example, would mean OR.) In this particular case, the /sbin/sysctl -p command will be executed only if the sysctl_modified class is set (that is, if /etc/sysctl.conf was modified) AND the no_restarts class is not set. This construct allows us to change the configuration files without executing any restart or reconfiguration commands, by defining the no_restarts class (which we could do, for example, by giving the -Dno_restarts command-line option to cf-agent when executing the policy).

This concludes the high-level description of the policy, which as you can see, describes in a fairly human-readable fashion what we want to achieve. In summary, our configuration file defines two bundles at the top level: configfiles() and edit_sysctl(). The configfiles() bundle provides the entry point for the policy, defines the files we want to edit and the contents we want them to have, and invokes the edit_sysctl() bundle (later in the chapter we will add calls to other bundles.) That bundle in turn carries out the edits we want to perform on the /etc/sysctl.conf file. Now we will delve deeper into the implementation details.

First, let's come back to the set_variable_values() bundle, since it seems so important. If you open cfengine_stdlib.cf, you will find its definition:

```
bundle edit_line set_variable_values(v) ❶
{
  vars:
      "index" slist => getindices("$(v)"); ❷
      "cindex[$(index)]" string => canonify("$(index)"); ❸
  field_edits: ❹
      "\s*$(index)\s*=.*" ❺
        edit_field => col("=","2","$($(v)[$(index)])","set"), ❻
        classes => if_ok("$(cindex[$(index)])_in_file"), ❼
        comment => "Match a line starting like key = something";
  insert_lines: ❽
      "$(index)=$($(v)[$(index)])",
        comment => "Insert a variable definition",
        ifvarclass => "!$(cindex[$(index)])_in_file";
}
```

Remember, from "Containers" on page 41, that bundles in CFEngine are equivalent to subroutines in other programming languages—they are self-contained units that can contain most different promise types, thus allowing us to encapsulate functionality. We will now dissect this set_variable_values() bundle to see how it performs its magic.

❶ This bundle receives as its argument, v, the *name* of an array. In our current example, the bundle will be invoked with v taking the value configfiles.sysctl, in which the indices are parameter names. The values in the array are the values to which the parameters will be set. So v provides the instructions to edit a file of the form name

= value, modifying the values of parameters that already exist, and adding those that do not exist yet.

❷ First, we get a list of all the parameters, and store it in the list variable named index. This is done using the built-in CFEngine function getindices() on the passed array, which returns a list of the indices in the array. Note that getindices() also receives the name of the array on which it will operate, so we can simply pass the $(v) parameter to it. (In CFEngine, you can use either braces or parenthesis around variable names; they are equivalent, so ${v} would mean the same.)

❸ Next, we generate an array of *canonified* parameter names. In CFEngine, a canonified string is a string that can be readily used as a class name. Because some characters are not valid in CFEngine class names, the CFEngine function canonify() allows us to take an arbitrary string and remove invalid characters from it. We store these canonified values in an array named cindex, indexed by the real parameter name so we can relate them to their canonified version. We use CFEngine's implicit looping to populate the entire array.

Implicit Looping in CFEngine

Although we have already described implicit looping in "Looping in CFEngine" on page 53, let us look in detail at what is going on in this variable assignment, to refresh your memory. If a list variable is referenced as a scalar (with the $ prefix instead of @), CFEngine automatically loops over all the values in the list, replacing each element in turn. Thus, by accessing the index array as a scalar ($(index) instead of @(index)), we are telling CFEngine to execute the corresponding statement once for every element of the array. In effect, the following line:

```
"cindex[$(index)]" string => canonify("$(index)");
```

will be repeated for every element of @(index), with $(index) taking each value in sequence. This results in the creation, element by element, of an array indexed by parameter names, and containing as values the canonified version of each name.

---

❹ The next step in performing the edits on the file is to update the values of parameters that already exist in the file. For this we use a field_edits: section, which also uses implicit looping to apply the editing promise for every parameter.

❺ The field_edits: promise starts with a regular expression that selects the lines in the file that need to have the edit applied. In this case, we want to edit any line that starts with the current parameter name ($(index)), surrounded by optional white-space (\s*), followed by an equals sign (=), and followed by an arbitrary string (we don't care about the existing value, since we will replace it with the new one). It is important to note that in field_edits: promises, CFEngine automatically anchors the given regular expressions to the beginning and end of the line, so the regex we give needs to match the whole line.

Notice again that thanks to CFEngine's implicit looping, this whole promise will be executed once for every single parameter stored in our `configfiles.sysctl` array. In our example, the array contains 5 elements, so the `field_edits:` promise will be evaluated 5 times, with `$(index)` iterating through the following values:

- `net.ipv4.tcp_syncookies`,
- `net.ipv4.conf.all.accept_source_route`,
- `net.ipv4.conf.all.accept_redirects`,
- `net.ipv4.conf.all.rp_filter`, and
- `net.ipv4.conf.all.log_martians`.

With a single promise and without any explicit flow-control instructions, CFEngine allows us to apply all of our edits to the whole file.

In this example we have a single promise inside the `field_edits:` section, but we could have several promises if we wanted to apply different types of field-based edits to the file.

❻ If any lines in the file match the regular expression (this is, that contain a definition of the given parameter), we will apply to them the changes defined by the `edit_field` attribute of the promise. For this we use yet another definition from the standard library called `col()`, and which allows generic field-based file editing. In this case, the arguments to `col()` tell it to use `=` as the field separator, and to `set` the second field of the line to the value given by the expression `"$($(v)[$(index)])"`.

There is a bit of variable interpolation magic going on here. Variable values in strings are expanded from the inside-out by CFEngine. First, the value of `$(v)` is expanded, so in our example the string will now read `$(configfiles.sysctl[$(index)])`. Next, the value of `$(index)` will be automatically iterated over each parameter value. As an example, for the `net.ipv4.tcp_syncookies` parameter, it will expand to `$(configfiles.sysctl[net.ipv4.tcp_syncookies])`. This now looks like a regular variable reference in CFEngine, which will give us the value we want to set for the given parameter, the string `"1"` in this case.

❼ If the promise is OK (in CFEngine, this means the promise was either already satisfied, or not satisfied but repaired), the `classes` attribute sets the `"$(cindex[$(index)])_in_file"` class. For example, if the parameter `net.ipv4.tcp_syncookies` already existed in the file, the `net_ipv4_tcp_syncookies_in_file` class will be set. This is the canonified version of the parameter name, concatenated with the string `_in_file`.

Remember from "Classes and Decision Making" on page 37 that *classes* in CFEngine are identifiers that are either set or unset, and that allow us to perform Boolean decisions. In this case, we are setting classes that contain the names of all the parameters that already existed in the file, whether their value was correct already or not. The existence of these classes indicates that there is no further work to be done for those particular parameters.

❽ If a parameter was not found in the file, it needs to be added, and this task is performed by the `insert_lines:` section of the bundle. The promiser in this case is the line we want to insert, in the form `parameter=value`, which promises to be inserted into the file *only if* the class expression given by the `ifvarclass` attribute is true. In this case, the value of `ifvarclass` is the negation (!) of the class defined by the `field_edits:` promise when the parameter was already present in the file. If the class is *not* defined (which means the parameter was not found in the file), the `ifvar class` expression evaluates to `true`, and the missing line will be inserted.

As an example, lets imagine that the `net.ipv4.conf.all.log_martians` parameter is not present in the file. Then the `field_edits:` promise will fail (because there is no line that matches the regular expression that searches for a line starting with the parameter name), and so the `net_ipv4_conf_all_log_martians_in_file` class will *not* be set. When the `insert_lines:` promise is executed, the value of the class expression `!$(cindex[$(index)])_in_file` (which expands to the string `!net_ipv4_conf_all_log_martians_in_file`) will be true, indicating that the line needs to be inserted.

You will notice this pattern of behavior often in CFEngine policies: doing some checks and fixes, setting certain classes based on the result, and then triggering other actions based on the existence of those classes. It seems convoluted at first, but it allows a lot of flexibility, and particularly allows policies to be convergent, not making changes unless they are necessary.

I must note that `insert_lines:` promises in CFEngine are quite smart. In particular, they will not insert a line that already exists in the file (this is a consequence of the promise theory underpinnings—if the line is already in the file, the promise has already converged to its desired state, and there is no need to insert it again), so in principle we should not need to set a class and then condition the insertion of the line on it. In this particular case, using the class allows us to account for things like spacing differences (e.g., spaces around the equals sign) that would not be considered by an unconditional `insert_lines:` promise.

To finish this discussion, we will go down one more level in the implementation chain, to discuss the three low-level body parts `if_repaired()`, `if_ok()`, and `col()`. None of these are native CFEngine functions, rather they are defined in the standard library as follows:

```
body classes if_repaired(x)
{
        promise_repaired => { "$(x)" };
}
body classes if_ok(x)
{
        promise_repaired => { "$(x)" };
```

```
        promise_kept => { "$(x)" };
}

body edit_field col(split,col,newval,method)
{
        field_separator     => "$(split)";
        select_field        => "$(col)";
        value_separator     => ",";
        field_value         => "$(newval)";
        field_operation     => "$(method)";
        extend_fields       => "true";
        allow_blank_fields  => "true";
}
```

 As a general rule, you should not worry too much about the implementation details of bundles in the standard library, just as you don't worry about the implementation details in the C standard library or in Perl CPAN modules. We are delving into the details here as an opportunity for you to learn more about the CFEngine policy language, and all the different levels at which it operates.

if_repaired() and if_ok() are both classes body parts, which means they can be used as the value of a classes attribute. This attribute is allowed in almost any CFEngine promise, and defines classes to be set depending on the result of the promise.

The two examples shown here should be fairly self-explanatory. In if_repaired(), we are specifying that the class whose name is given as argument $(x) will be defined only when the promise was repaired (this is, when some change had to be made in order to bring the promise to its desired state). In if_ok(), we are specifying that the class will be defined when the promise was either repaired or kept (this is, it was already true). We examined the col() body in detail in "Bodies" on page 45. In this case we are specifying the field separator, the field to be selected for edition, its value, and the operation to be performed.

This finishes our explanation for now. I would like to remind you of the different levels of abstraction present even in this simple example:

1. At the highest level (configfiles() bundle), the policy simply says "configure the /etc/sysctl.conf file."

2. The next level (edit_sysctl bundle), says "set these values in the /etc/sysctl.conf file."

3. The next level (set_variable_values() bundle) explains the structure of the file and how the parameters should be set.

4. The lowest level (col(), if_ok(), if_repaired()) explains how to perform the field edits in the file, how classes should be handled, and other implementation details.

The beauty of CFEngine is that you need to work only at the level of abstraction that is needed at the moment. In fact, different sets of people could operate at each level. A policy maker could set the requirements at the highest level (even higher than the levels shown here, in fact), and both system administrators and CFEngine administrators could operate at the lower levels as required.

Editing /etc/sshd_config

Another common task upon initial installation of a system is to configure certain services, SSH (Secure Shell) being a particularly useful one, and OpenSSH being one of the most popular SSH implementations. By default, the OpenSSH daemon ships with a fairly usable configuration, but you may still want to change it to be more secure, or to adhere to local policies.

Having seen how to edit /etc/sysctl.conf in the previous section, you should already start to see how to perform this configuration. For the sake of our example, let's say we want to modify the following parameters in /etc/ssh/sshd_config from their default configuration in an OpenSSH installation:

```
#Protocol 1,2
#X11Forwarding no
#UseDNS yes
```

In OpenSSH, most configuration parameters appear commented out by default, showing their default values. We would like to modify these parameters to the following:

```
Protocol 2
X11Forwarding yes
UseDNS no
```

This is, we want to uncomment the corresponding lines, and modify their values to the ones we want. If the line for the parameter we want does not exist already, we want to add it to the configuration file.

With this in mind, we can rewrite our earlier top-level configfiles() bundle to the following:

```
bundle agent configfiles
{
  vars:
      # Files to edit
      "files[sysctl]" string => "/etc/sysctl.conf";
      "files[sshd]"   string => "/etc/ssh/sshd_config";

      # Sysctl variables to set
      "sysctl[net.ipv4.tcp_syncookies]"                string => "1";
      "sysctl[net.ipv4.conf.all.accept_source_route]"  string => "0";
      "sysctl[net.ipv4.conf.all.accept_redirects]"     string => "0";
      "sysctl[net.ipv4.conf.all.rp_filter]"            string => "1";
      "sysctl[net.ipv4.conf.all.log_martians]"         string => "1";

      # SSHD configuration to set
      "sshd[Protocol]"                                 string => "2";
      "sshd[X11Forwarding]"                            string => "yes";
      "sshd[UseDNS]"                                   string => "no";
```

```
methods:
    "sysctl"  usebundle => edit_sysctl;
    "sshd"    usebundle => edit_sshd;
}
```

You can see that we added a second element to the files array, files[sshd], which contains the path of the */etc/ssh/sshd_config* file. We have also added a new array called sshd, containing the parameters we want to set in the configuration file. Finally, in the methods: section, we added a call to an edit_sshd() bundle, which performs the necessary edits. Note again the very clear separation that CFEngine allows in specifying *what to do* (the values of the parameters that we want to set) from *how to do it* (the methods: calls, and their respective implementations). Here is the new edit_sshd() bundle:

```
bundle agent edit_sshd
{
  files:
    "$(configfiles.files[sshd])"
      handle => "edit_sshd",
      comment => "Set desired sshd_config parameters",
      edit_line => set_config_values("configfiles.sshd"),
      classes => if_repaired("restart_sshd");

  commands:
    restart_sshd.!no_restarts::
    "/etc/init.d/sshd reload"
      handle => "sshd_restart",
      comment => "Restart sshd if the configuration file was modified";
}
```

The edit_sshd() bundle is very similar to edit_sysctl(), except that instead of calling the set_variable_values() bundle for editing the file (which is used to set lines of the form variable=value) we use the set_config_values() bundle, which is used to set lines of the form variable value, with the additional feature of automatically uncommenting lines if they exist already in commented-out form.

The edit_sshd() bundle also has a commands: section, which is used to restart the *sshd* daemon if the configuration file was changed. As before, we set the restart_sshd class if the file-editing promise was repaired (that is, if any changes were made to the file), and depending on this class, we issue the necessary command.

Let us now look at the set_config_values() bundle, also defined in the standard library.

```
bundle edit_line set_config_values(v)
{
  vars:
    "index" slist => getindices("$(v)"); ❶
    "cindex[$(index)]" string => canonify("$(index)");
  replace_patterns: ❷
    "^\s*($(index)\s+(?!$($(v)[$(index)])).*|# ?$(index)\s+.*)$"
      replace_with => value("$(index) $($(v)[$(index)])"), ❸
      classes => always("replace_attempted_$(cindex[$(index)])"); ❹
```

```
insert_lines:
    "$(index) $($(v)[$(index)])" ❺
        ifvarclass => "replace_attempted_$(cindex[$(index)])";
}
```

This bundle uses a completely different logic from set_variable_values(), even though
it performs similar functions. This allows me to introduce you to a couple of new concepts and tricks.

❶ The first part of the bundle is already familiar: it gets a list of indices from the array
passed to the bundle, stores it in index, and uses it to populate cindex with the
canonified versions of those parameter names, to be used in class names later.

❷ The actual line editing is done now by a replace_patterns: section instead of
field_edits:, which allows for more flexible transformations. Promises of this type
allow us to search for and replace regular expressions in the file.

The promiser in a replace_patterns: promise is the regular expression we want to
match. In this case we are asking it to look for two types of lines, corresponding to
the two regular expressions separated by a pipe character (|):

1. Lines that start (^) with optional whitespace (\s*), followed by the current parameter name ($(index)) followed by whitespace (\s+) and any string that is not
   the correct value of the current parameter ((?!$($(v)[$(index)])).*). This rep-
   resents lines that already set the parameter we are looking for, but with an incorrect value.

2. Lines that start (^) with optional whitespace (\s*), followed by a comment
   character and an optional space (# ?), followed by the current parameter name
   ($(index)) followed by whitespace (\s+) and any arbitrary string. This represents
   lines that contain the parameter, but commented out.

Again, we are using implicit looping to iterate over all the parameters to be set, by
using $(index) instead of @(index) in the promise.

The last part of the first regular expression is complicated because we need to find
lines that do not contain the correct value already, and replace them. For this, we
use a negative-lookahead expression ((?!...)) that indicates that the text after the
whitespace must not match the desired value ((?!$($(v)[$(index)]))). The final
part (.*) is necessary to match the actual characters that follow the whitespace,
because the whole negative-lookahead expression is zero-length, and does not "con-
sume" any characters during the regex evaluation.

❸ The replace_with attribute tells us what to use as the replacement. In this case, the
replacement will be the current parameter and its desired value, separated by a space:

```
replace_with => value("$(index) $($(v)[$(index)])"),
```

value() is another compound body that specifies the value and characteristics of the
replacement text. It is defined in the standard library:

```
body replace_with value(x)
{
        replace_value => "$(x)";
        occurrences => "all";
}
```

❹ For reasons I will explain in a moment, we want to remember that the
`replace_patterns:` promise has run, whether or not it actually found its pattern. So
it ends by setting the `replace_attempted_`*parameter* class using the `classes` attribute
with the `always()` body part. The definition of the `always()` body part is also found
in *cfengine_stdlib.cf*:

```
body classes always(x)
{
        promise_repaired => { "$(x)" };
        promise_kept => { "$(x)" };
        repair_failed => { "$(x)" };
        repair_denied => { "$(x)" };
        repair_timeout => { "$(x)" };
}
```

The effect of using `always()` is that the class given as a parameter is set for any of the
conditions listed in it (`promise_repaired`, `promise_kept`, `repair_failed`,
`repair_denied` or `repair_timeout`). These are all the possible outcomes of a promise
in CFEngine, so the net effect is to set the class regardless of what has happened.

❺ Up to this point we have dealt with parameters whose lines are already in the file
(maybe commented out), but we also need to insert parameters that do not yet
appear in the file. How to do this is a little tricky and counter-intuitive, but it gives
us an opportunity to learn more about how CFEngine works.

As we saw in "Normal Ordering" on page 51, promise sections in a CFEngine policy
are executed in a hard-coded sequence known as *normal ordering*. According to
normal ordering, the `insert_lines:` section is executed *before* the
`replace_patterns:` section. This poses a problem in our current example because
we want to try to fix already-existing parameters (possibly commented out or with
incorrect values) *before* adding any new lines. If we let the `insert_lines:` promise
execute first, we may end up with duplicated definitions of parameters in the configuration file.

Normal Ordering in edit_line Bundles

Within `edit_line` bundles, the sections are executed, up to three times, in the following order: `vars`, `classes`, `delete_lines`, `field_edits`, `insert_lines`,
`replace_patterns` and `reports`.

To alter the order of execution, we condition the execution of the `insert_lines:`
promise on the existence of the `replace_attempted_`*parameter* class defined when the
`replace_patterns:` promise is evaluated. Because CFEngine does up to three passes

over the promises, this makes the `insert_lines:` promise execute only on the second pass, after the `replace_patterns:` section has had a chance to uncomment and correct any existing lines. If at this point the line with the correct value *still* does not exist, then inserting it is the correct behavior.

I know this can be confusing, so here is an example to clarify it. Suppose that our */etc/ssh/sshd_config* file contains the following line:

```
#Protocol 1,2
```

The behavior of the `set_config_values()` bundle will be the following (assuming `$(index)` currently has the value `"Protocol"`):

1. (First pass) The `insert_lines:` promise for `"Protocol 2"` is not executed because the `replace_attempted_protocol` class is not defined. Note that the class name contains the *canonified* version of the parameter name, which includes making it all lowercase.

2. (First pass) The `replace_patterns:` promise replaces the original line with its uncommented, correct value, and defines the `replace_attempted_protocol` class:

```
Protocol 2
```

3. (Second pass) The `insert_lines` promise now executes, but because the correct line is already present in the file, it is not inserted again.

Now consider the case when the commented-out `"Protocol"` line is not present at all in the file. Then the flow would be the following:

1. (First pass) The `insert_lines` promise for `"Protocol 2"` is not executed because the `replace_attempted_protocol` class is not defined.

2. (First pass) The `replace_patterns` promise is executed but does not succeed because the line does not exist. It defines the `replace_attempted_protocol` class anyway, due to the use of the `always()` body.

3. (Second pass) The `insert_lines` promise now executes, and because the line `"Protocol 2"` does not exist in the file, it is inserted.

In both cases, the end result is the same: to set the `Protocol` parameter to its correct value. It is important to note that our previously-examined `set_variable_values()` bundle could trivially be rewritten using the same technique used by `set_config_values()`, which would add the functionality of allowing it to handle commented-out lines properly.

 Note that the example we saw in this section assumes each parameter can only appear once in the file. This assumption does not hold true if the file contains "Match" blocks, which allow specifying conditional configuration values. In the interest of clarity I have considered only the simplest example in the book. For the full functionality, please see the networking/ssh sketch in the CFEngine Design Center (*https://github.com/cfengine/design-center/tree/master/networking/ssh*).

Editing /etc/inittab

Another common initial task when setting up a Unix or Linux system is to customize */etc/inittab*. For our example, we will do the following tasks:

1. Modify the default runlevel from 5 to 3, to disable graphical login by default (this is commonly done on Linux servers, to prevent wasting resources on an unused graphical console).

2. Disable Ctrl-Alt-Del handling, to prevent this key combination from rebooting the system.

To achieve the first task, we need to modify the second field in the following line:

```
id:5:initdefault:
```

This is a fairly simple task, now that you understand the previous editing tasks we have done. Here is the promise that achieves it:

```
files: ❶
    "/etc/inittab"
      handle => "inittab_set_initdefault",
      comment => "Ensure graphical mode is disabled (default runmode=3)",
      create   => "false",
      edit_defaults => backup_timestamp, ❷
      edit_line => set_colon_field("id","2","3"); ❸
```

❶ This is a `files:` promise that indicates the file to edit, and states that the file must not be created (`"create" => "false"`) if it does not exist already, since */etc/inittab* should always exist in a Unix system.

❷ The `edit_defaults` attribute specifies the behavior for the file-editing operation. The definition of `backup_timestamp` can be found in the standard library:

```
body edit_defaults backup_timestamp
{
      empty_file_before_editing => "false";
      edit_backup => "timestamp";
      max_file_size => "300000";
}
```

This states that the file should not be emptied before editing (you can set this to true when the promise will recreate the file in its entirety), that a copy of the old version should be kept, named with a timestamp at the end (this allows you to keep a history of the file, and is particularly advisable for critical system files, so that you can quickly revert any changes if problems arise), and that the file should not be more than 300,000 bytes in size (this is simply a sanity check to ensure that files do not grow beyond normal limits).

You will notice that we had omitted the `edit_defaults` attribute in our previous file-editing promises. This is valid and provides sane default behavior. We use `edit_defaults` now in particular because it is a good idea to keep backup copies of the */etc/inittab* file in case anything goes wrong.

❸ The actual editing of */etc/inittab* is done by the standard library `set_colon_field()` bundle, which allows us to edit fields in a colon-separated file. Here is its definition:

```
bundle edit_line set_colon_field(key,field,val)
{
  field_edits:
    "$(key):.*"
      comment => "Edit a colon-separated file, using the first field as a key",
      edit_field => col(":","$(field)","$(val)","set");
}
```

This bundle uses the same lower-level `col()` body we employed in "Editing /etc/sysctl.conf" on page 69, only this time using the colon as a separator to set the appropriate field to the value we provide. As used in our promise, `col()` results in the second field of the line whose first field is "id" to be set to "3".

To achieve the second task, we need to comment out the following line:

```
ca::ctrlaltdel:/sbin/shutdown -r -t 4 now
```

We can use the following promise to achieve this:

```
files:
    "/etc/inittab"
      handle => "inittab_disable_ctrlaltdel",
      comment => "Ensure handling of ctrl-alt-del is disabled",
      create     => "false",
      edit_defaults => backup_timestamp,
      edit_line => comment_lines_matching("ca::ctrlaltdel:.*", "#");
```

Again, the actual work in this promise is performed by the `edit_line` attribute, which in this case calls the `comment_lines_matching()` bundle. This standard library bundle is used to insert a comment character (given as the second argument, in this case "#") at the beginning of any line that matches the first argument. Here it its definition:

```
bundle edit_line comment_lines_matching(regex,comment)
{
  replace_patterns:
    "^($(regex))$"
      replace_with => comment("$(comment)"),
      comment => "Search and replace string";
}
```

It consists, as you might have expected, of a simple `replace_patterns:` promise. The replacement string is defined by the `comment` compound body definition, which is also in the standard library:

```
body replace_with comment(c)
{
    replace_value => "$(c) $(match.1)";
    occurrences => "all";
}
```

In the `replace_value` attribute, `$(c)` is the comment string we passed as an argument, and `$(match.1)` refers to the content of the first set of parenthesis in the regular expression used to select the line. If you look back in the comment_lines_matching() bundle, you'll see that the regular expression is given as "^($(regex))$", which has grouping parenthesis that capture the whole matched line. This results in the matching line being replaced by the comment character, followed by a space, and then the previous content of the line.

Putting it all together, and extending our previous configfiles() bundle to handle editing the */etc/inittab* file, we get the following:

```
bundle agent configfiles
{
  vars:
      # Files to edit
      "files[sysctl]" string => "/etc/sysctl.conf";
      "files[sshd]" string => "/etc/ssh/sshd_config";
      "files[inittab]"    string => "/etc/inittab";

      # Sysctl variables to set
      "sysctl[net.ipv4.tcp_syncookies]"             string => "1";
      "sysctl[net.ipv4.conf.all.accept_source_route]" string => "0 ";
      "sysctl[net.ipv4.conf.all.accept_redirects]"   string => "0";
      "sysctl[net.ipv4.conf.all.rp_filter]"          string => "1";
      "sysctl[net.ipv4.conf.all.log_martians]"       string => "1";

      # SSHD configuration to set
      "sshd[Protocol]"                              string => "2";
      "sshd[X11Forwarding]"                         string => "yes";
      "sshd[UseDNS]"                                string => "no";

  methods:
      "sysctl"  usebundle => edit_sysctl;
      "sshd"    usebundle => edit_sshd;
      "inittab" usebundle => edit_inittab;
}

bundle agent edit_inittab
{
  files:
      "$(configfiles.files[inittab])"
        handle => "inittab_set_initdefault",
        comment => "Ensure graphical mode is disabled (default runmode=3)",
        create => "false",
        edit_defaults => backup_timestamp,
        edit_line => set_colon_field("id","2","3");

      "$(configfiles.files[inittab])"
        handle => "inittab_disable_ctrlaltdel",
        comment => "Ensure handling of ctrl-alt-del is disabled",
        create => "false",
        edit_defaults => backup_timestamp,
        edit_line => comment_lines_matching("ca::ctrlaltdel:.*", "#");
}
```

Here, we have simply moved the filename into the `files` array that we have been using, and added the call to `edit_inittab()` to the `methods:` section.

Configuration Files with Variable Content

So far, we have been making fixed changes to configuration files, which is helpful enough, but CFEngine is able to handle much more complex situations. In a real network not all systems are the same, and you have a mixture of operating systems, releases, and parameters that affect how each machine should be configured. Handling these almost-the-same-but-slightly-different configurations by hand is a certain recipe for disaster: eventually, someone will lose track of the changes that have to be made, forget to make certain changes, or make the wrong set of changes, and a system will stop working. With CFEngine, these configurations can be made consistently and without errors.

Class-based configuration

CFEngine automatically discovers a large amount of information about the system and its current state and sets classes based on them. These are called *hard classes* in CFEngine terminology because they are set by CFEngine based on system characteristics; they are different from *soft classes*, which are set by the policy during its execution. Using hard classes, we can instruct CFEngine to act differently depending on characteristics of each system or of the moment when CFEngine is executed.

To know which classes are discovered by CFEngine, we can use the *cf-promises* command like this:

```
# cf-promises -v -f /var/cfengine/inputs/failsafe.cf | grep Defined
nova> -> Defined classes = { 10_123_6_61 32_bit Day19 Friday
GMT_Hr3 Hr03 Hr03_Q1 Lcycle_0 Min05 Min05_10 Night November
PK_SHA_1d71f214f33a57877c602ee2436e467f846c0d03e27809d6261a3781fcc7d16d
Q1 SLES11 SuSE Yr2010 any cfengine_3 cfengine_3_1 cfengine_3_1_0
common compiled_on_linux_gnu ec2_internal i686 internal cfhost1
cfhost1_ec2_internal ipv4_10 ipv4_10_123 ipv4_10_123_6
ipv4_10_123_6_61 linux linux_2_6_32_19_0_3_ec2 linux_i686
linux_i686_2_6_32_19_0_3_ec2
linux_i686_2_6_32_19_0_3_ec2__1_SMP_2010_09_17_20_28_21__0200
net_iface_eth0 net_iface_eth1 nova_edition verbose_mode xen
xen_domu_pv }
```

Let's look at some of these classes and what the names tell us:

- Time information is given by classes such as `Day19` (19th of the month), `Friday`, `Hr3` (3AM), `Min05_10` (it's between 3:05 and 3:10), `Hr03_Q1` and `Q1` (the current quarter-hour), `Night` (it's at night), `November`, `Yr2010`, `Lcycle_0` (this is a "lifecycle index" defined as the year modulo 3, and which can be used for long-term scheduling). All times are expressed in the local timezone.

- Network information is given by classes such as 10_123_6_61 (the host's IP address), ipv4_10, ipv4_10_123, ipv4_10_123_6, ipv4_10_123_6_61 (the different portions of the IP address), net_iface_eth0 and net_iface_eth1 (the network interfaces defined in the system)

- System information is given by classes such as cfhost1 (the host name), cfhost1_ec2_internal (its FQDN, with the dots replaced by underscores), linux, SuSE, SLES11 (operating system type and, in this case, Linux distribution information), i686 (system architecture), linux_2_6_32_19_0_3_ec2 (Linux kernel version and build information), xen (it's a Xen virtual machine).

- CFEngine information is given by classes such as cfengine_3, cfengine_3_1, cfengine_3_1_0 (version number), nova_edition (CFEngine edition), PK_SHA_1d71... (the cryptographic signature of the host's cfengine-generated public key, which can be used to uniquely identify the system), verbose_mode (which tells us CFEngine was run with the -v option, so you could tie your own verbose output to the use of this option).

Hard classes allow a great deal of flexibility in writing configurations by offering very detailed factors on which you can hang changes. You rarely have to define a new class in order to distinguish a machine for special handling.

As an example, you could use the system type to decide which command to use for a certain task:

```
bundle agent reboot
{
  commands:
    linux::
      "/sbin/shutdown -r now";
    windows::
      "c:/Windows/system32/shutdown.exe /r /t 01";
}
```

Remember that in CFEngine, lines that end with a double colon are interpreted as *class expressions*, which indicate that the lines that follow should be evaluated only if the expression evaluates to true. In this case the selection is very simple: we use one command for rebooting Linux systems, and a different one for Windows machines, using the hard classes linux and windows as class expressions.

We can also combine classes in more complex expressions. Extending our previous example, we could use the *and* (. or &) operator to condition a reboot on both the existence of the reboot_needed class and the corresponding operating-system class. Additionally, we can produce an error if the machine is *not* (!) Linux *and* (.) *not* (!) Windows (we can use parenthesis for grouping parts of the expression):

```
bundle agent reboot
{
  commands:
    reboot_needed.linux::
      "/sbin/shutdown -r now";
```

```
reboot_needed.windows::
    "c:/Windows/system32/shutdown.exe /r /t 01";

reports:
  reboot_needed.!(linux|windows)::
    "I know how to reboot only Linux and Windows machines.";
}
```

Time-based classes can be used to emulate cron-like behavior using CFEngine. For example:

```
bundle agent cron_tasks
{
  commands:
    Min00_05::    # Commands to run hourly
      "/usr/sbin/updatedb";
    Hr00::        # Commands to run daily at different times
      "/usr/local/sbin/logrotate";
      "/usr/sbin/tmpclean";
    Hr03::
      "/usr/local/sbin/run_backups";
    Monday::      # Commands to run weekly
      "/usr/sbin/usercheck";
    Lcycle_0::    # Commands to run every four years
      "/usr/sbin/random_catastrophic_failure";
}
```

In a bundle like this, you can define any number of tasks to execute. The best part is that thanks to CFEngine's locking mechanisms, you do not have to worry about executing a command multiple times: if the command has already been executed according to the current conditions, it will not be executed again (unless you run *cf-agent* with the -K option, which instructs CFEngine to ignore all the internal locks). The other big advantage is that using CFEngine as a cron replacement allows you to schedule not only commands and shell scripts, but also arbitrary CFEngine promises, which you can use to perform more complex tasks than you could using cron alone.

System-information classes allow you to perform different tasks depending on the system state or configuration. For example, you could easily create different network profiles using CFEngine:

```
bundle agent network_profiles
{
  commands:
    # At home, 192.168.23.0/24, start my backup
    ipv4_192_168_23::
      "/usr/local/sbin/open_services.sh";
      "/usr/local/sbin/run_backup.sh";
      "/usr/local/sbin/configure_home_printer.sh";
    # At work, 9.4.0.0/16, configure the appropriate printers
    ipv4_9_4::
      "/usr/local/sbin/open_services.sh";
      "/usr/local/sbin/configure_work_printers.sh";
    # Anywhere else, close some services for additional protection
    !(ipv4_192_168_23|ipv4_9_4)::
```

```
        "/usr/local/sbin/close_services.sh";
   }
```

In this case, we are modifying system settings based on the IP address range in which the system is currently configured. The possibilities are endless.

System-state-based configuration

Another, even more flexible, way of configuring a system involves using its current state to determine the desired end state, making the policy fully dynamic depending on each particular system.

In one of my projects, we had a large number of Linux machines with two network interfaces, one of them connected to the production network (which we called the "green" network) and the other one to the management network (called the "black" network). Due to the characteristics of the networking infrastructure, we had to disable the TSO flag (TCP Segmentation Offload) on the interfaces that were on the green network. In my first attempt at automating this, I observed that the green interface was always eth0 (these were all Linux systems), and hard-coded the CFEngine configuration to add the following line to /etc/inittab:

```
tso:3:once:/usr/sbin/ethtool -K eth0 tso off
```

This results in the *ethtool* command being run upon system boot to disable this flag. The policy to achieve this is very similar to the ones we have seen before, so I will not show its exact implementation.

This worked fine... until exceptions started to appear: systems in which the green interface was not necessarily eth0. Then the rules had to adapt, and with CFEngine this was fairly simple to accomplish.

In this particular case, the two networks could be easily identified by their IP address ranges. The green network was in the 192.168.0.0/16 range, and the black network was in the 10.10.0.0/16 range. With this piece of information, I was able to modify the policy so that the correct interface is used in the *ethtool* command. Here is the complete bundle:

```
bundle agent disable_tso_flag
{
  vars:
      "ipregex" string => "192\.168\..*"; ❶
      "nics"    slist  => getindices("sys.ipv4");

  classes:
      "isgreen_$(nics)" expression => regcmp("$(ipregex)", "$(sys.ipv4[$(nics)])"); ❷

  files: ❸
      "$(configfiles.files[inittab])"
        handle => "inittab_add_ethtool",
        comment => "Ensure ethtool is run on startup to disable the TSO flag",
        create => "false",
        edit_defaults => edit_backup,
```

```
        edit_line => replace_or_add("tso:3:.*", ❹
                                    "tso:3:once:/usr/sbin/ethtool -K $(nics) tso off"),
        ifvarclass => "isgreen_$(nics)";
}
```

This bundle is meant to be incorporated into the main policy that we have been developing throughout this chapter, since it refers to the configfiles() bundle. Let's examine it in more detail.

❶ First, we assign to the $(ipregex) variable the regular expression to select the interfaces we want (the green ones, in this case). Next, we store in the @(nics) list the indices of the special CFEngine array sys.ipv4. This is a special variable created by CFEngine that contains all the IP addresses configured in the system, indexed by interface name. Therefore, getindices("sys.ipv4") gives us a list of all the network interfaces on the system.

❷ Once we have this list, we again make use of CFEngine's implicit looping to assign a number of classes named isgreen_*ifname*, where *ifname* represents each of the network interfaces on the system. Each class is true if the IP address of said interface, given by the value "$(sys.ipv4[$(nics)])" matches $(ipregex) (remember that $ (nics) is set to each of the interface names in turn). So, for example, if the system has the following network interfaces:

- eth0: 9.4.21.16
- eth1: 189.177.231.225
- eth2: 192.168.13.56
- eth3: 10.10.54.25

then the evaluation of the classes will be as follows:

- isgreen_eth0: unset
- isgreen_eth1: unset
- isgreen_eth2: **set**
- isgreen_eth3: unset

This tells us exactly which interface is the one we need to use in the *ethtool* command.

❸ Armed with this knowledge, we can proceed to the files: promise, which adds to */etc/inittab* the line that executes the *ethtool* command. This command contains the interface name as given by the $(nics) variable (implicit looping in action again), *only* if the corresponding isgreen_*ifname* class is set, as indicated by the ifvarclass => "isgreen_$(nics)" clause in the promise.

❹ To actually append the line we use another bundle from standard library called replace_or_add that does the following: if a line matches the regular expression given by the first argument, it is replaced in its entirety by the second argument. If no match is found, the line given in the second argument is added to the file. The replace_or_add bundle is very simple. It uses the same trick as the set_config_values bundle we discussed before (setting a class unconditionally upon execution of the replace_patterns: promise) to achieve the desired operation:

```
bundle edit_line replace_or_add(pattern,line)
{
  vars:
      "cline" string => canonify("$(line)");
  replace_patterns:
      "^(?!$(line)$)$(pattern)$"
        replace_with => value("$(line)"),
        classes => always("replace_done_$(cline)");
  insert_lines:
      "$(line)"
        ifvarclass => "replace_done_$(cline)";
}
```

It pays to know the built-in classes (*http://cf-learn.info/ref/hard-classes*), variables (*http://cf-learn.info/ref/special-variables*) and functions (*http://cf-learn.info/ref/special-functions*) in CFEngine, since they help achieve most necessary processing and data extraction tasks. I would strongly encourage you to read through the corresponding sections in the reference manual to get familiar at least in general terms with the available functionality.

We have described the use of CFEngine's implicit looping several times. This concept isn't found in most programming languages, so it can be hard to wrap your head around it at the beginning. Once you get the hang of it, you will realize that it can save many lines of flow-control code that would be necessary in other languages, and whose absence in CFEngine allows you to focus on writing the policy. In fact, CFEngine goes out of its way to *prevent* you from worrying about the flow of execution in a policy, using concepts such as implicit looping and normal ordering to determine how things are executed.

It is a natural tendency at the beginning to fight this level of automation, but true CFEngine mastery lies in letting go of the urge to control everything down to the last detail, and using CFEngine the way it is meant to be used. Tell CFEngine what you want and how to do it, and let CFEngine worry about details like the order in which operations will be executed.

User Management

One of the basic tasks of any system administrator is to control user accounts. Whether they are local accounts or centralized accounts using some network-wide mechanism such as LDAP, CFEngine gives you the exact control you need.

From a high-level perspective, the definition of user accounts may be expressed as follows:

```
bundle agent manage_users
{
  vars:
```

```
# Users to create
"users[root][fullname]"   string => "System administrator";
"users[root][uid]"        string => "0";
"users[root][gid]"        string => "0";
"users[root][home]"       string => "/root";
"users[root][shell]"      string => "/bin/bash";
"users[root][flags]"      string => "-o -m";
"users[root][password]"   string => "FkDMzhB1WnOp2";

"users[zamboni][fullname]"  string => "Diego Zamboni";
"users[zamboni][uid]"       string => "501";
"users[zamboni][gid]"       string => "users";
"users[zamboni][home]"      string => "/home/zamboni";
"users[zamboni][shell]"     string => "/bin/bash";
"users[zamboni][flags]"     string => "-m";
"users[zamboni][password]"  string => "dk52ia209rfuh";

    methods:
        "users"    usebundle => create_users("manage_users.users");
    }
```

This example stores the user characteristics in a two-dimensional array indexed by username and by the different fields of each user record. The create_users() bundle is called from the methods: section of the policy, passing the configuration array as an argument. Here is the create_users() bundle:

```
bundle agent create_users(info)
{
  vars:
      "user"         slist => getindices("$(info)");  ❶

  classes:
      "add_$(user)"  not => userexists("$(user)");  ❷

  commands:  ❸
    linux::
      "/usr/sbin/useradd $($(info)[$(user)][flags]) -u $($(info)[$(user)][uid])
       -g $($(info)[$(user)][gid]) -d $($(info)[$(user)][home])
       -s $($(info)[$(user)][shell]) -c '$($(info)[$(user)][fullname])' $(user)"
          ifvarclass => "add_$(user)";
    windows::
      "c:/Windows/system32/net user $(user) $($(info)[$(user)][password]) /add
      \"/fullname:$($(info)[$(user)][fullname])\" \"/homedir:$($(info)[$(user)][home])
\""
          ifvarclass => "add_$(user)";
      # On Windows we use a command to set the password
      # unconditionally in case it has changed.
      "c:/Windows/system32/net user $(user) $($(info)[$(user)][password])";  ❹

  files:
    linux::
      # This is not conditioned to the add_* classes
      # to always check and reset the passwords if needed.
      "/etc/shadow"  ❺
        edit_line => set_user_field("$(user)", 2, "$($(info)[$(user)][password])");
```

```
    reports: ❻
      !linux.!windows::
        "I only know how to create users under Linux and Windows.";
      verbose_mode::
        "Created user $(user)"
          ifvarclass => "add_$(user)";
}
```

This particular implementation of create_users() handles only local user accounts, both on Linux and on Windows.

❶ In the vars: section, we store in @(user) a list of the user accounts to check (the top-level indices of the configuration array) using the getindices() function. This list is used through CFEngine's implicit looping to apply the rest of the bundle to each of those accounts.

❷ The classes: section defines a class named add_*username* for each user account that does not exist, by using the built-in userexists() function to check for the existence of each user in turn.

The userexists() function does not return valid results on Windows when using the community edition of CFEngine, but it does work properly if you are using one of the commercial editions. Proper Windows support is one of the benefits of the commercial versions of CFEngine.

Note that we are using implicit looping again, but this time the variable $(user) is being used in two places: as part of the classname, and as argument to the userexists() function.

❸ The commands: section is divided by operating systems, using the predefined OS-type hard classes provided by CFEngine. Here, we issue the necessary command-line instructions to create the users, but only if the user does not exist already. This is controlled by the ifvarclass attribute added to each command promise, which makes the statement execute only if the given class expression is true.

Note that the other account attributes (other than the password, see below) are not verified for accuracy, in this version of the bundle. If the account exists already, the promise is considered as satisfied.

❹ Since we also want to enforce the passwords for each account, we have to make sure the passwords are checked and, if needed, changed every time.

In the case of Windows, we issue the command to reset the password to its desired value every time the policy runs. This is done from the commands: section. (In this case, the password has to be given in clear text in the users array.)

❺ For Linux, we reset user passwords in the `files:` section, by directly editing the */etc/shadow* file to set the password field to the value given in the user matrix (this value has to be desired password, already encoded using the `crypt()` function appropriate for the operating system). The `set_user_field()` bundle can be found in the standard library, and is very similar to the `set_colon_field()` function I described before.

❻ Finally, the `reports:` section produces a report for each user that was created, if verbose mode is enabled (the `verbose_mode` class is automatically set when the `-v` command-line option is given to *cf-agent*), and also an error if we are running on an unsupported system.

The call to `manage_users()` could be easily integrated into the overarching `configfiles()` bundle we have been building, by adding one more line to the `methods:` section:

```
"users"   usebundle => manage_users;
```

To make things easier to manage, we could also get rid of `manage_users()` entirely, move the definition of the user accounts from the `manage_users()` bundle to the `configfiles()` bundle, where all our other user-configurable variables are being set, and call `create_users()` directly:

```
bundle agent configfiles
{
  vars:
    ...
      # Users to create
      "users[root][gecos]"      string => "System administrator";
      "users[root][uid]"        string => "0";
      "users[root][gid]"        string => "0";
      "users[root][home]"       string => "/root";
      "users[root][shell]"      string => "/bin/bash";
      "users[root][flags]"      string => "-o -m";
      "users[root][password]"   string => "FkDMzhB1WnOp2";

      "users[zamboni][gecos]"    string => "Diego Zamboni";
      "users[zamboni][uid]"      string => "501";
      "users[zamboni][gid]"      string => "users";
      "users[zamboni][home]"     string => "/home/zamboni";
      "users[zamboni][shell]"    string => "/bin/bash";
      "users[zamboni][flags]"    string => "-m";
      "users[zamboni][password]" string => "dk52ia209rfuh";

  methods:
    ...
      "users"   usebundle => create_users("configfiles.users");
}
```

This is a very simple example that manages only local accounts, but which is useful, for example, to set known attributes on common local accounts such as root. However, CFEngine has the ability to manage much more complex scenarios, including centralized user directories. LDAP integration (including Active Directory) is properly supported in the commercial editions of CFEngine.

Software Installation

One of the main tasks of system maintenance is the installation, configuration, upgrading, and removal of software. In old times, most software on a system was (a) part of the operating system, installed or upgraded whenever the whole system was installed or upgraded, (b) commercial software that had its own installation mechanisms, or (c) open-source software that had to be compiled and installed manually. Over time, most operating systems have developed package-management mechanisms, which make it easier to install and manage software of any kind. Unfortunately, package-management mechanisms vary wildly in their capabilities and user interfaces, which makes writing software that can interface with any of them a daunting task. Furthermore, there is still the need (however sporadic) to compile and install software manually.

CFEngine provides powerful and generic mechanisms for dealing with this task, that make it possible to adapt it to the needs of every particular system.

Package-Based Software Management

CFEngine understands package management as a generic concept. Each package is represented by three attributes: its name, its version, and its architecture. CFEngine allows you to perform operations such as add, delete, and update. The specifics of how to interact with the package-management system are abstracted into discrete components of the policy, and can be customized to interact with any command-line-driven package manager.

All package-management promises in CFEngine occur in the packages: section of an agent bundle. CFEngine allows us to make promises about the state of the packages in the system, and leaves the work of actually modifying the packages to the underlying packaging system. Keep in mind that given the widely varying capabilities of package management systems, we must take their capabilities into consideration when writing package-management promises (for example, if the system uses rpm, we should take into account that it will not automatically fetch and install dependencies of the package being installed).

Let us look at a very simple example:

```
bundle agent software
{
  vars:
      "pkgs" slist => {
                        "subversion",
                        "tcpdump"
                      };
  packages:
```

```
        "$(pkgs)"
          package_policy => "addupdate",
          package_method => apt;    # For Debian and Ubuntu
    }
```

We define a list variable containing the packages we want to install or update (Subversion and tcpdump), and use them in a promise that specifies the addupdate package policy, which means "update the package if it's installed, install it if not." We also specify apt as the package method, which is the package management system in Debian-based Linux distributions.

Some standard package_method bodies, including apt, are defined in the standard library. Let us look at its definition (some lines have been wrapped for readability):

```
body package_method apt
{
        package_changes => "bulk";
        package_list_command => "/usr/bin/dpkg -l"; ❶
        package_list_name_regex    => "ii\s+([^\s]+).*"; ❷
        package_list_version_regex => "ii\s+[^\s]+\s+([^\s]+).*";
        package_installed_regex => ".*"; # all reported are installed
        package_name_convention => "$(name)"; ❸

        # set it to "0" to avoid caching of list during upgrade
        package_list_update_ifelapsed => "240";

    have_aptitude:: ❹
        package_add_command => "/usr/bin/env
          DEBIAN_FRONTEND=noninteractive LC_ALL=C
          /usr/bin/aptitude -o Dpkg::Options::=--force-confold
          -o Dpkg::Options::=--force-confdef --assume-yes install";
        package_list_update_command => "/usr/bin/aptitude update";
        package_delete_command => "/usr/bin/env
          DEBIAN_FRONTEND=noninteractive LC_ALL=C
          /usr/bin/aptitude -o Dpkg::Options::=--force-confold
          -o Dpkg::Options::=--force-confdef --assume-yes -q remove";
        package_update_command =>  "/usr/bin/env
          DEBIAN_FRONTEND=noninteractive LC_ALL=C
          /usr/bin/aptitude -o Dpkg::Options::=--force-confold
          -o Dpkg::Options::=--force-confdef --assume-yes install";
        package_verify_command =>  "/usr/bin/aptitude show";
        package_noverify_regex =>
          "(State: not installed|E: Unable to locate package .*)";

    !have_aptitude::
        package_add_command => "/usr/bin/env
          DEBIAN_FRONTEND=noninteractive LC_ALL=C
          /usr/bin/apt-get -o Dpkg::Options::=--force-confold
          -o Dpkg::Options::=--force-confdef --yes install";
        package_list_update_command => "/usr/bin/apt-get update";
        package_delete_command => "/usr/bin/env
          DEBIAN_FRONTEND=noninteractive LC_ALL=C
          /usr/bin/apt-get -o Dpkg::Options::=--force-confold
          -o Dpkg::Options::=--force-confdef --yes -q remove";
        package_update_command =>  "/usr/bin/env
```

```
                        DEBIAN_FRONTEND=noninteractive LC_ALL=C
                        /usr/bin/apt-get -o Dpkg::Options::=--force-confold
                        -o Dpkg::Options::=--force-confdef --yes install";
                    package_verify_command => "/usr/bin/dpkg -s";
                    package_noverify_returncode => "1";
    }
```

A package_method body tells CFEngine how to execute the commands that actually perform the operations, and how to process their output to obtain necessary information:

❶ The package_list_command attribute specifies the command to run to generate a list of packages on the system.

❷ Coupled with this, the package_list_name_regex and package_list_version_regex attributes tell CFEngine the regular expressions to apply on the output of the package-listing command to determine each package's name and version. Additionally, the package_installed_regex is used to determine which of the packages in the listing are actually installed (in this case, because of the command used, all packages in the output are installed, but this may not be the case in other package-management systems).

❸ The package_name_convention attribute tells CFEngine how to specify a package when executing any of the commands. Some package-management systems may require both the name and the version to operate. *apt* needs only the name, hence it's specified like this.

❹ The have_aptitude class is a hard class that CFEngine defines automatically on Debian-like systems when the *aptitude* package management program is installed, since it provides some additional capabilities. Depending on this class, the body sets the specific commands for adding, removing or updating packages.

The standard library includes predefined package_method bodies for several common package managers, including *zypper*, *apt*, *rpm*, *yum*, Windows MSI installers, the Solaris package manager and the FreeBSD package manager. There is also a generic package method that combines all of the above, and provides the correct values according to the appropriate operating-system hard classes.

It is important to note that a package_method definition specifies exactly how to interact with the package manager, and thus allows you to interact with any packaging mechanism you want by writing the appropriate package_method. Useful examples of this would be package_method definitions for popular language-specific or tool-specific package managers, such as Pear (*http://pear.php.net/*) or Ruby Gems (*http://rubygems.org/*).

Package promises can be far more complicated. The name, version, and architecture attributes can be used in package promises to define the desired result. We can also use version-comparison operators to further refine the actions. For example:

```
bundle agent software
{
  vars:
      "version[openssl]"  string => "0.9.8k-7ubuntu8";
      "version[ssl-cert]" string => "1.0.23ubuntu2";

      "architectures" slist => { "x86_64" };
      "allpkgs"       slist => getindices("version");

  packages:
      "$(allpkgs)"
        package_policy => "add",
        package_select => "==",
        package_version => "$(version[$(allpkgs)])",
        package_architectures => @(architectures),
        package_method => apt;    # For Debian and Ubuntu
}
```

In this case, we are using an array to store the versions we want, indexed by package name. Then we are using the list of indices from the array to install the specific version we want for each package, also specifying the desired architecture. We are again using an array and implicit looping to request the needed version for each one of the packages. The package_select attribute with value "==" tells CFEngine that we want exactly the specified version of the package (by default its value is ">=", which gives us the latest available version older than the one specified).

When package_policy is verify (this is its default value), all that CFEngine does is check that the desired packages are installed correctly. This can be used to simply report on the correctness of the system, without attempting to fix anything[1]. For example:

```
bundle agent verify_packages
{
  vars:
      "allpkgoutput" string => execresult("/usr/bin/rpm -qa --queryformat \"%{name}\n
\"");
      "allpkgs"       slist => splitstring("$(allpkgoutput)", "\s+", 999999);

  packages:
      "$(allpkgs)"
        package_policy => "verify",
        package_method => rpm,
        classes => if_notkept("incorrect_$(allpkgs)");

  reports:
      "Problem: package $(allpkgs) is not installed correctly."
        ifvarclass => "incorrect_$(allpkgs)";
}
```

This bundle starts by getting the listing of all packages by running an external command using the execresult() function, and storing it in the $(allpkgoutput) string, which

---

1. The concept of "verify" is dependent on the package manager, and some package_method bodies do not support it.

then gets split by the `splitstring()` function into the `@(allpkgs)` list. We then iterate over this list verifying each package in turn. If the promise is not kept (this is, if the package does not get verified correctly), the `packages` bundle defines a `incorrect_pack agename` class. In the `reports:` section, we iterate again over `@(allpkgs)`, printing a message for the packages whose `incorrect_packagename` class is defined. We can use this as a general "sanity check" of a system, for example to produce a report of its current state if we have a new system that comes under our management, or to trigger automatic corrective actions.

Manual Software Management

Although package management software is the ideal way to install and uninstall software on a system, there may be cases in which you want or need to manage software manually. One such case would be when the software you need to install is not available in your operating system's software repository, or if you need to compile or install it in a custom way, or if you need a specific version that is too old or too new to be in the repository.

In this section we develop a CFEngine policy to manually install an application. This requires more manual work and each policy will be unique to the application that is being installed, so you may want to minimize the number of applications you install using this method. However, it is useful to know how to perform this task for the times when it is needed.

For our example, we will install the WordPress (*http://wordpress.org/*) blogging and CMS application. From the WordPress documentation, we can see that it has a fairly simple installation procedure (*http://codex.wordpress.org/Installing_WordPress#De tailed_Instructions*):

1. Install the system requirements: Apache, PHP, and MySQL;
2. Download and extract the package;
3. Create a MySQL database and user to use with WordPress;
4. Set up `wp-config.php` with the necessary database parameters, using `wp-config-sample.php` as a starting point.

These steps give us a fairly good guide for implementing the installation using CFEngine. We'll create a `wp_install` bundle, but let's start by thinking how we would like to invoke it:

```
body common control
{
        bundlesequence => { wp_install("g.wp_config") };
        inputs => { "cfengine_stdlib.cf", "wordpress.cf" };
}

bundle common g
{
```

```
vars:
    "wp_config[DB_NAME]"      string => "wordpress";
    "wp_config[DB_USER]"      string => "wordpress";
    "wp_config[DB_PASSWORD]"  string => "lopsa10linux";
debian::
    "wp_config[_htmlroot]"    string => "/var/www";
redhat::
    "wp_config[_htmlroot]"    string => "/var/www/html";
any::
    "wp_config[_wp_dir]"      string => "$(wp_config[_htmlroot])/blog";
}
```

We are defining, in the common g bundle, the wp_config array with our parameters for the installation. The most important parameters are the database name, user and password, and the directory where we want WordPress to be installed. Note that we use classes to assign a different value to the htmlroot parameter depending on whether we are on a Debian or a RedHat system, to account for slight differences between those distributions.

The wp_install() bundle is called directly from the bundlesequence declaration, passing the name of the configuration array as a parameter. The wp_install() bundle could also be called, for example, from the methods: section of some other bundle, as we did before in our configfiles() bundle.

Let's now walk through the actual implementation of the wp_install policy.[2]

1. The wp_install() bundle is the point of entry for this policy bundle, which calls all other tasks:

```
bundle agent wp_install(params)
{
  methods:
      "wp_vars"  usebundle => wp_vars("$(params)");
      "wp_pkgs"  usebundle => wp_packages_installed("wp_vars.conf");
      "wp_svcs"  usebundle => wp_services_up("wp_vars.conf");
      "wp_tar"   usebundle => wp_tarball_is_present("wp_vars.conf");
      "wp_xpnd"  usebundle => wp_tarball_is_unrolled("wp_vars.conf");
      "wp_mysql" usebundle => wp_mysql_configuration("wp_vars.conf");
      "wp_cfgcp" usebundle => wp_config_exists("wp_vars.conf");
      "wp_cfg"   usebundle => wp_is_properly_configured("wp_vars.conf");
}
```

This bundle receives as argument a variable called params, which must contain *the name of an array* that itself contains the different adjustable parameters of this bundle, such as the database user and password to use (as in the sample invocation we saw before, the argument was the string "g.wp_config"; this is how we have passed configuration arrays before: by using their name instead of passing the array itself). In the first methods: call to the wp_vars() bundle, the configuration array is extended with default parameter values (for those that are not specified by the

---

2. This policy was originally written by Aleksey Tsalolikhin. It is available in the CFEngine Design Center (*https://github.com/cfengine/design-center*) and is used with permission.

user), and with some hard-coded internal parameters related to the operation of the bundle, such as the file into which the *wordpress.tar.gz* file will be downloaded, the URL from where it will be fetched, the path of the *service* command, and the name by which the Apache web server is identified. The extended parameter array is stored in `wp_vars.conf`, which will be used by all the other bundles (we will examine in detail the operation of the `wp_vars()` bundle in "Passing Name-Value Pairs to Bundles" on page 126). In the rest of the `methods:` section of this bundle, we call the other bundles that actually perform the required tasks. The `wp_vars.conf` array is passed to every single bundle. In `methods:` promises, the promiser is an arbitrary string that (at least in current CFEngine versions) is not used for any purpose. For clarity, we use short identifiers for each of the methods we are calling.

2. The first step of the actual installation process is to make sure all WordPress pre-requisites are properly installed and working. This is taken care of by two bundles, `wp_packages_installed()` and `wp_services_up()`. The first one uses the native package-management facilities to install the prerequisites for WordPress:

```
bundle agent wp_packages_installed(params)
{
  vars:
    debian::  ❶
      "desired_package" slist => {
                                   "apache2",
                                   "php5",
                                   "php5-mysql",
                                   "mysql-server",
                                 };
    redhat::
      "desired_package" slist => {
                                   "httpd",
                                   "php",
                                   "php-mysql",
                                   "mysql-server",
                                 };
    packages:  ❷
      "$(desired_package)"
        package_policy => "add",
        package_method => generic,
        classes => if_repaired("packages_added");

  commands:
    packages_added::  ❸
      "$($(params)[_sys_servicecmd]) $($(params)[_sys_apachesrv]) graceful"
        comment => "Restarting httpd so it can pick up new modules.";

}
```

❶ We first define the list of necessary packages for each operating system that we want to support.

❷ This is then used in the packages: section of the bundle to install them as appropriate. If any of the package promises are *repaired* (this means, if any of the packages need to be installed), the packages_added class will be defined.

❸ If the packages_added class is defined, Apache needs to be restarted to ensure it uses any newly-available modules. The path of the *service* command and the name of the service to restart (httpd in RedHat, apache2 in Debian) are taken from the params array as defined in wp_vars().

The wp_services_up() bundle ensures that both MySQL and Apache are running:

```
bundle agent wp_services_up(params)
{
  processes:
    debian:: ❶
      "/usr/sbin/mysqld" restart_class => "start_mysqld";
      "/usr/sbin/apache2"  restart_class => "start_httpd";
    redhat::
      "^mysqld" restart_class => "start_mysqld";
      "^httpd"  restart_class => "start_httpd";

  commands: ❷
    start_mysqld::
      "$($(params)[_sys_servicecmd]) mysql start";

    start_httpd::
      "$($(params)[_sys_servicecmd]) $($(params)[_sys_apachesrv]) start" ;
}
```

❶ First we ensure that both mysqld and httpd are running by using a processes: section. Different process-matching strings are used depending on the Linux distribution used, due to the differences in how the processes appear in the process table. If any of the processes are not running, the corresponding restart_class is defined.

❷ If any of the restart classes are defined (start_mysqld or start_httpd), the corresponding command is run to start the appropriate service.

After both of these bundles are called from the methods: section of the main wp_install() bundle, both the HTTP and MySQL daemons will be running, with the appropriate modules installed.

3. Next, we need to download the WordPress distribution file if it is not present already. This is taken care of by the wp_tarball_is_present() bundle:

```
bundle agent wp_tarball_is_present(params)
{
  classes: ❶
    "wordpress_tarball_is_present"
      expression => fileexists("$($(params)[_tarfile])");

  commands: ❷
    !wordpress_tarball_is_present::
```

```
                "/usr/bin/wget -q -O $($(params)[_tarfile]) $($(params)[_downloadurl])"
                  comment => "Downloading latest version of WordPress.";

        reports: ❸
          wordpress_tarball_is_present::
            "WordPress tarball is on disk.";
    }
```

❶ In the classes: section we define a class depending on the existence of the tar file that contains the WordPress distribution. The location and filename of this file is also contained in the params configuration array.

❷ If the class is not defined (which means the file is not present), the commands: section uses the *wget* command to download the file to the proper location.

❸ If the file was already there, we don't download it again, and simply report its existence in the reports: section.

4. Once we ensure that the WordPress distribution file is present, the wp_tarball_is_unrolled() bundle makes sure it has been expanded:

```
    bundle agent wp_tarball_is_unrolled(params)
    {
        classes: ❶
            "wordpress_src_dir_is_present"
              expression => fileexists("$($(params)[_htmlroot])/wordpress");
            "wordpress_final_dir_is_present"
              expression => fileexists("$($(params)[_wp_dir])");

        reports:
          wordpress_final_dir_is_present::
            "WordPress directory is present.";

        commands:
          !wordpress_final_dir_is_present&!wordpress_src_dir_is_present:: ❷
            "/bin/tar -xzf $($(params)[_tarfile])"
              comment => "Unroll WP tar to $($(params)[_htmlroot])/wordpress.",
              contain => in_dir_shell("$($(params)[_htmlroot])");
          wordpress_src_dir_is_present&!wordpress_final_dir_is_present::
            "/bin/mv $($(params)[_htmlroot])/wordpress $($(params)[_wp_dir])"
              comment => "Rename unrolled directory to destination $($(params)[_wp_dir])";
    }
```

This bundle is very similar to the previous one, except that:

❶ The existence check is done on the directory into which the tar file expands, contained in the _wp_dir parameter of the configuration array.

❷ If it does not exist, we use the *tar* command to expand it under the directory defined by the _htmlroot parameter. This will create a directory named *wordpress* under that directory, since that is how the WordPress tar file is packaged. After unpacking the distribution, we rename the resulting wordpress directory to its final name as indicated by the _wp_dir parameter, from where it will be served by the web server.

5. Once the files are in place, it is time to configure WordPress, and the first step is creating a MySQL database and user for WordPress to use. This is done by the wp_mysql_configuration() bundle:

```
bundle agent wp_mysql_configuration(params)
{
  commands:
      "/usr/bin/mysql -u root -e \"
      CREATE DATABASE IF NOT EXISTS $($(params)[DB_NAME]);
      GRANT ALL PRIVILEGES ON $($(params)[DB_NAME]).*
      TO '$($(params)[DB_USER])'@localhost
      IDENTIFIED BY '$($(params)[DB_PASSWORD])';
      FLUSH PRIVILEGES;\"
  ";
}
```

This is a very simple bundle: it just runs the *mysql* command-line utility with the appropriate SQL commands to perform the task. In this respect, MySQL makes things quite easy, since a single command can be used to create the database if it doesn't exist already, create the user if it doesn't exist already, and set the user password.

6. The second bundle involved in configuring WordPress is wp_config_exists():

```
bundle agent wp_config_exists(params)
{
  classes:
      "wordpress_config_file_exists"   ❶
        expression => fileexists("$($(params)[_wp_config])");

  files:
    !wordpress_config_file_exists::   ❷
      "$($(params)[_wp_config])"
        copy_from => backup_local_cp("$($(params)[_wp_cfgsample])");

  reports:
    wordpress_config_file_exists::
      "WordPress config file $($(params)[_wp_config]) is present";
    !wordpress_config_file_exists::
      "WordPress config file $($(params)[_wp_config]) is not present";
}
```

❶ This bundle first checks whether the *wp-config.php* file already exists inside the WordPress installation directory. If it does, we do not want to overwrite it, since it may already have some customizations (this is useful when updating Word-Press to a new version).

❷ If the file does not exist, the wordpress_config_file_exists class will not be set, and in this case the files: section will create it using the *wp-config-sample.php* file shipped with WordPress as the starting point.

7. After making sure the configuration file is in its proper place, we want to ensure that it contains the appropriate parameters. For this we use the wp_is_properly_configured() bundle:

```
bundle agent wp_is_properly_configured(params)
{
  vars:
      "allparams" slist => getindices("$(params)"); ❶
    secondpass::
      "wpparams"  slist => grep("[^_].*", "allparams");

  classes:
      "secondpass" expression => isvariable("allparams");

  files:
      "$($(params)[_wp_config])" ❷
        edit_line =>
          replace_or_add(
          "define\('$(wpparams)', *(?!'$($(params)[$(wpparams)]))')'.*",
          "define('$(wpparams)', '$($(params)[$(wpparams)])')');");
}
```

Although this is a short bundle, there is a lot going on behind the scenes, so let us take a moment to understand what it does.

❶ First, we store in the allparams list the indices of the configuration array that is passed into the bundle as the params argument. This gives us, according to the definition given in our example, the following values:

```
{ DB_NAME, DB_USER, DB_PASSWORD, _htmlroot, _tarfile, ... }
```

We then use the grep() built-in function to select from allparams only those parameters that do not start with an underscore, to avoid storing internal parameters in the WordPress configuration file. The filtered list is stored in wpparams, which would have in our example the following values:

```
{ DB_NAME, DB_USER, DB_PASSWORD }
```

Due to an artifact of the way variables are converged in the current version of CFEngine, we need to use a trick to make sure the wpparams list is assigned only on the *second pass* of the CFEngine policy evaluation (remember that CFEngine makes three passes over each bundle). Not doing this results in the wpparams list being empty, because it is filled using the original value of allparams and not the final value obtained using the getindices() function. To achieve this, we set class second pass in the classes: section based on whether the allparams variable exists, and in the vars: section, wpparams is only created when the secondpass class is true. For details about how this works, see "Controlling Promise Execution Order" on page 138.

❷ To understand the trick we are about to use, we need to look at the lines in the *wp-config.php* file that we want to modify:

```
/** The name of the database for WordPress */
define('DB_NAME', 'database_name_here');

/** MySQL database username */
define('DB_USER', 'username_here');

/** MySQL database password */
define('DB_PASSWORD', 'password_here');
```

Notice that we have used, as the indices in the `wp_config` array, the same parameter names used in the *wp-config.php* file (plus some others, which we use internally in the policy). This allows the `edit_line` statement in the `files:` section to do its magic using CFEngine's implicit looping (you should by now be getting the idea that this is one of the most powerful features in CFEngine!). In this statement, we replace the following regexp:

```
define\('$(wpparams)', *(?!'$($(params)[$(wpparams)]))'.*
```

by the following text:

```
define('$(wpparams)', '$($(params)[$(wpparams)])');
```

Through implicit looping, `$(wpparams)` takes the value of each index in sequence. So, for example, when `$(wpparams)` has the value `DB_NAME`, the regular expression looks like this:

```
define\('DB_NAME', *(?!'$($(params)[DB_NAME]))'.*
```

and the replacement string looks like this:

```
define('DB_NAME', 'wordpress');
```

 The negative look-ahead (?!...) in the regular expression is used to match only lines in which the correct value is not already present, and to ensure the proper convergence of the replacement operation. Without this, CFEngine notices that the regular expression matches the line even after the replacement operation has taken place, and considers it to be a non-properly-convergent operation. It still works, but will produce a warning from CFEngine every time it runs.

This means, we will replace whatever value the `DB_NAME` parameter has at the moment with the correct one, taken from the `wp_config` array. If the line does not exist at all, it will be added to the file. This will happen for all the parameters in that array automatically, and the file will be rewritten to disk only if at least one change is actually made to it. A nice side effect of this automation is that we can modify any parameter in the *wp-config.php* file just by adding a new element to the configuration array. For example, if we needed to set the

DB_CHARSET parameter, all we need to add is the following line to the definition of wp_config:

```
"wp_config[DB_CHARSET]"  string => "iso8859-1";
```

There are a few aspects of this configuration to focus on. First, I would like to draw a contrast between this policy and a shell script that would perform the same tasks. The main difference is that in a CFEngine policy, we simply specify the end state we want to achieve (for example, a directory or a file existing), and CFEngine only proceeds with the actions if any aspects of the system are not in the desired state.

Second, notice that we are making use of some of the generic tools and tricks that we have built elsewhere, or that are available in the standard libraries. For example, we use the replace_or_add() bundle from standard library to edit the WordPress configuration file. And we are using an array to pass parameters, which allows us to do some generic manipulations and traversing of the data, as seen in the wp_is_properly_configured() bundle.

Third, note how using the methods: section allows us to break a task into sub-tasks, thereby providing a single point of entry (in this case, the wp_install() bundle) into a policy that may be arbitrarily complex.

In general, I would advise you to use the built-in package management facilities for handling software in the system, using the interfaces that CFEngine provides to these systems. However, as we have just seen, it is entirely possible to perform ad-hoc software installation and configuration when needed. These are tasks that, when managing systems manually, you would have to perform anyway. CFEngine allows you to automate and perform them in the best possible way. As your mechanism to install and configure the software improves (or, for example, when the package appears in a proper way in the software repository), your CFEngine policy can evolve to adapt to your needs and possibilities. For example, when WordPress becomes available in the software repository, you could keep wp_install() as the main entry point for the policy, and simply replace the first five calls in the methods: section by a single call to a bundle that handles the installation using packages: promises.

Using CFEngine for Security

A large part of maintaining security in a computer system consists of maintaining proper configuration of the systems, which makes CFEngine well suited for the task of configuring, maintaining, and monitoring security-related state. In this section we will explore some of the applications of CFEngine in this area.

Policy Enforcement

Many organizations have security policies that are in turn translated into specific configuration specifications for computer systems. While CFEngine cannot help with mapping high-level policies into procedures and implementations, it can certainly make sure that the implementations are correctly applied and maintained. Here are some example security-related policies that are common in some systems, and how CFEngine can help in enforcing them. In the process we will learn and revisit some CFEngine concepts and constructs.

Login banners

This is a simple one. CFEngine can make sure a login banner is always present, and contains the approved text according to the policy. For example:

```
body common control
{
        bundlesequence => { "login_banner" };
        inputs => { "cfengine_stdlib.cf" };  ❶
}

bundle agent login_banner
{
  vars:
      "template_file" string => "/var/cfengine/templates/motd_template.txt";   ❷
      "motd_file"     string => "/etc/motd";

  files:
      "$(motd_file)"   ❸
        handle => "set_login_banner",
        comment => "Ensure the login banner is set to the authorized text",
        create => "true",
        perms => mog("644", "root", "wheel"),
        edit_defaults => empty,
        edit_line => expand_template("$(template_file)");  ❹
}
```

In this example we are making use of CFEngine's template-expanding mechanism to populate the */etc/motd* file with the appropriate content. Let us examine what is going on.

❶ First, we must include the CFEngine standard library, since the policy makes use of several bodies and bundles defined in it.

❷ We store in variables the filenames of the template file, and of the actual file to be edited. This is not needed, but it is a good practice to have all user-defined values in a single, differentiated place. We will look at the contents of the template file in a moment.

❸ In the `files:` promise we tell CFEngine, among other things, that the */etc/motd* file needs to be created if it doesn't exist, that it needs to have permissions 644 (or rw-r--r--), belong to user `root` and group `wheel`, and that it should be emptied completely before inserting the lines. For these specifications we use two bodies from the standard library, namely:

```
body perms mog(mode,user,group)
{
        owners => { "$(user)" };
        groups => { "$(group)" };
        mode   => "$(mode)";
}

body edit_defaults empty
{
        empty_file_before_editing => "true";
        edit_backup => "false";
        max_file_size => "300000";
}
```

Both of these bodies are very simple. The first one simply passes on the permissions it receives, and the second simply specifies that the file must be emptied before starting the editing. Remember that CFEngine does all the editing in memory and writes results to the disk only if they are different from what was there before, so there are no unnecessary edits of the file, even when empty_file_before_editing is used.

❹ The edit_line attribute is the one that actually specifies how the file will be edited. We have seen in previous examples how to add and delete lines, how to search and replace using regular expressions, and how to edit field-based files. Now we will use yet another file-editing facility provided by CFEngine, that of using templates for specifying the contents of a file. This is the expand_template() bundle from the standard library:

```
bundle edit_line expand_template(templatefile)
{
  insert_lines:
      "$(templatefile)"
        insert_type => "file",
        comment => "Expand variables in the template file",
        expand_scalars => "true";
}
```

This bundle contains an insert_lines: promise like those we have seen before, but in this case the insert_type attribute has the value "file", which indicates that the promiser is to be interpreted not as the text to insert, but rather as a file whose contents will be inserted. The promiser in this case is the $(templatefile) variable passed as an argument. This means that the contents of this file will be inserted. Additionally, the expand_scalars attribute indicates that the content of the file will be scanned for variable references, and those variables will be expanded before inserting the text.

The template file could contain something like this:

```
This system may be accessed by authorized users only.
Use of this system implies acceptance of authorized use policies.
Misuse may be subject to prosecution.
```

```
Host: $(sys.fqhost) ($(sys.ipv4))
This system is managed by CFEngine v$(sys.cf_version)
This file was generated from $(login_banner.template_file)
```

Variables in the template are referenced just as you would in any other string. Keep in mind that all variables in the template must be referenced with their full module path, as shown in the reference to the login_banner.template_file variable.

Template files are a powerful mechanisms for generating files using CFEngine. They make it easier to modify the contents of a file without having to touch the policy files that maintain it, and make it easier to understand what the final contents of the file will be without having to untangle the logic of the code.

Password expiration periods

Password expiration is another common configuration policy that is mandated by security policies, and which is possible to set and maintain using CFEngine. For example, in Linux systems this is commonly done using the /etc/login.defs file. We can use the following bundle to set these parameters appropriately:

```
bundle agent password_expiration
{
  vars:
      # Maximum password age
      "logindefs[PASS_MAX_DAYS]"                    string => "180";    ❶
      # Minimum password age (minimum days between changes)
      "logindefs[PASS_MIN_DAYS]"                    string => "10";
      # Warning period (in days) before password expires
      "logindefs[PASS_WARN_AGE]"                    string => "5";

      # Position of each parameter in /etc/shadow
      "fieldnum[PASS_MIN_DAYS]"  string => "4";   ❷
      "fieldnum[PASS_MAX_DAYS]"  string => "5";
      "fieldnum[PASS_WARN_AGE]"  string => "6";

      # List of parameters to modify
      "params" slist => getindices("logindefs");   ❸

      # UIDs below this threshold will not be touched
      "uidthreshold" int => "500";   ❹
      # Additionally, these users and UIDs will not be touched.
      # These are comma-separated lists.
      "skipped_users" string => "vboxadd,nobody";   ❺
      "skipped_uids"  string => "1000,1005";

      # Get list of users, and also generate them in canonified form
      "users" slist => getusers("$(skipped_users)", "$(skipped_uids)");   ❻
      "cusers[$(users)]" string => canonify("$(users)");

  classes:
      # Define classes for users that must not be modified,
      # either by UID threshold or by username
      "skip_$(cusers[$(users)])"  expression => islessthan(getuid("$(users)"),   ❼
```

```
                                                       "$(uidthreshold)");

    files:
        "/etc/login.defs"    ❽
          handle => "edit_logindefs",
          comment => "Set desired login.defs parameters",
          edit_line => set_config_values("password_expiration.logindefs");

        "/etc/shadow"    ❾
          handle => "edit_shadow_$(params)",
          comment => "Modify $(params) for individual users.",
          edit_defaults => backup_timestamp,
          edit_line => set_user_field("$(users)",
                                      "$(fieldnum[$(params)])",
                                      "$(logindefs[$(params)])"),
          ifvarclass => "!skip_$(cusers[$(users)])";
}
```

The idea is to set in */etc/login.defs* new default values for the minimum and maximum password ages, as well as the warning period to users when the password expiration date is approaching. To ensure consistency, we also edit */etc/shadow* to change all user-specific expiration settings to the default value. But we don't want to blindly change all the user entries, because this would most certainly cause problems by changing the password periods for system accounts such as root, lpd, or daemon. To address this, we include a system for excluding certain users by user ID threshold (all UIDs below a set threshold are ignored), and also by specific usernames and user IDs. This bundle brings together several concepts we have discussed before and introduces a couple of new ideas. Let us look in detail at how it works:

❶ We set the value we want for each of the parameters. The parameter names (the array indices) are the names as they appear in */etc/login.defs*. In this case, we want to set a maximum password lifetime of 180 days, a minimum of 10 days between password changes, and a warning period of 5 days before the password expires.

❷ Like we said, we need to set these parameters also in */etc/shadow* for preexisting users. For this reason, we define the field number in which each parameter appears in this file. This will allow us to make the promise that edits */etc/shadow* generic as well.

❸ The list variable @(params) holds the list of parameters whose values we want to set, obtained automatically from the logindefs array. Defining this list will allow us to write generic file-editing promises, as we will see in a moment.

❹ We now get to the definition of the exceptions. First we define $(uidthreshold), which contains the minimum User ID for which changes in */etc/shadow* will be applied. (In this case, all users with UID smaller than 500 will be skipped. This includes most system and application users.)

❺ Continuing with the exceptions, we define $(skipped_users) and $(skipped_uids), both of which contain comma-separated lists of usernames and user IDs to skip.

This is meant to allow more fine-grained control over users whose parameters should not be modified.

The exception definitions are combined: both users with a UID lower than $(uid threshold), *and* those listed in $(skipped_users) or $(skipped_uids), will be skipped when making changes.

❻ We get a list of all the users in the system using the built-in function getusers(). This function returns a list of users and takes two parameters, which allow us to specify lists of users and UIDs that should not be returned, so we use our two variables $(skipped_users) and $(skipped_uids) directly. We store the list of users in the @(users) list variable.

Additionally, we generate a list of canonified usernames, and store them in the cusers array. Most usernames should be safe to use in class names, but it's better to do this conversion anyway to have the certainty that they will not produce errors.

❼ In the classes: section of the policy, we finally start applying the logic of the policy to decide which users must be skipped. For this, we make use one more time of CFEngine's implicit looping to create per-users classes named skip_*username*. The class is defined using the built-in function islessthan() to compare the user ID of the current user (the current username is contained in $(users) by the magic of implicit looping, and its user ID is obtained using the getuid() function) against the threshold defined in the $(uidthreshold) variable. The class skip_*username* will be defined for all those users for which the condition is true.

Finally, by this point we have the list of users to edit, the list and values of the parameters to modify, and all the per-user classes to tell us which users need to be skipped. Now we will apply these pieces of information into editing */etc/login.defs* and */etc/shadow*.

❽ We use a files: promise to edit the values in */etc/login.defs*. This is a fairly simple promise: we use the set_config_values() bundle just like we did in "Editing /etc/sshd_config" on page 78.

❾ The second files: promise does the editing of /etc/shadow for all users in the system. Note that this promise is parameterized using the $(params) variable, which means that in practice it is evaluated as three promises: one for each element of @(params). Note that we use $(params) even in the handle and comment of the promise, so that we can clearly identify which parameters failed.

The promise also loops over all the available users, thanks to the reference to the $(users) variable. The ifvarclass attribute indicates that only those users for which the skip_*username* class is not defined will be examined.

The editing work is done, as usual, by the edit_line attribute. This attribute tells CFEngine that the corresponding field for each parameter (as indicated by $(fieldnum[$(params)])) must be set to the correct value, as stored in

$(logindefs[$(params)]). The set_user_field() bundle comes from the standard library.

Security Scanning

Let us now look at another way to use CFEngine as a security tool. A common strategy is to establish mechanisms to detect unwanted file changes—in fact one of the oldest and most respected security tools, Tripwire, does precisely this, and is the centerpiece of a successful business venture. CFEngine can also perform monitoring for file changes. CFEngine keeps cryptographic hash values for all the files it manages in order to detect changes that may trigger certain actions (for example, the file may need to be re-copied from a remote server, or fixed in some way). The trick is to leverage this database to focus on change detection as the end objective.

Looking at the CFEngine reference manual, we find that there exists a changes attribute to files: promises. It is defined as a compound body, which means it needs to be declared as an external body part. It looks promising, since it supports the following attributes: hash, report_changes, update_hashes and report_diffs.

The standard library is a good source for learning how to use different CFEngine constructs, and in this case it doesn't disappoint. Looking for "body changes" definitions, we find the following little gem:

```
body changes detect_all_change
{
        hash          => "best";
        report_changes => "all";
        update_hashes => "yes";
}
```

This seems to be exactly what we need. And indeed, it is all we need if we only want to monitor a single file. For example:

```
bundle agent monitor_files
{
  vars:
      "files" slist => { "/bin/ls", "/etc/passwd", "/etc/motd" };

  files:
      "$(files)"
        changes => detect_all_change;
}
```

This simple bundle allows us to define an arbitrary list of files to monitor in the @(files) list, and will produce an alert when one of them changes. The first time you run it, you will see something like this, as CFEngine adds the hashes of the files to its database:

```
# cf-agent -KI -f ./monitor_one_file.cf
 !! File /bin/ls was not in md5 database - new file found
I: Report relates to a promise with handle ""
```

```
I: Made in version 'not specified' of './monitor_one_file.cf' near line 14
 !! File /bin/ls was not in sha1 database - new file found
I: Report relates to a promise with handle ""
I: Made in version 'not specified' of './monitor_one_file.cf' near line 14
 !! File /etc/passwd was not in md5 database - new file found
I: Report relates to a promise with handle ""
I: Made in version 'not specified' of './monitor_one_file.cf' near line 14
 !! File /etc/passwd was not in sha1 database - new file found
I: Report relates to a promise with handle ""
I: Made in version 'not specified' of './monitor_one_file.cf' near line 14
 !! File /etc/motd was not in md5 database - new file found
I: Report relates to a promise with handle ""
I: Made in version 'not specified' of './monitor_one_file.cf' near line 14
 !! File /etc/motd was not in sha1 database - new file found
I: Report relates to a promise with handle ""
I: Made in version 'not specified' of './monitor_one_file.cf' near line 14
```

Afterward, if any of the files is modified, CFEngine will produce the appropriate alerts:

```
# echo "Hello world" >> /etc/motd
# cf-agent -KI -f ./monitor_one_file.cf
!!!!!!!!!!!!!!!!!!!!!!!!!!!!!!!!!!!!!!!!!!!!!!!
ALERT: Hash (md5) for /etc/motd changed!
!!!!!!!!!!!!!!!!!!!!!!!!!!!!!!!!!!!!!!!!!!!!!!!
 -> Updating hash for /etc/motd to MD5=49e27c52055d818c4632195289102b9d
I: Report relates to a promise with handle ""
I: Made in version 'not specified' of './monitor_one_file.cf' near line 14
!!!!!!!!!!!!!!!!!!!!!!!!!!!!!!!!!!!!!!!!!!!!!!!
ALERT: Hash (sha1) for /etc/motd changed!
!!!!!!!!!!!!!!!!!!!!!!!!!!!!!!!!!!!!!!!!!!!!!!!
 -> Updating hash for /etc/motd to SHA=9de806f39f914ba8b209f03121c395f4ee8956fb
I: Report relates to a promise with handle ""
I: Made in version 'not specified' of './monitor_one_file.cf' near line 14
!!!!!!!!!!!!!!!!!!!!!!!!!!!!!!!!!!!!!!!!!!!!!!!
ALERT: Last modified time for /etc/motd changed Sun Nov  6 08:17:42 2011 ->
  Sun Nov  6 08:22:37 2011
!!!!!!!!!!!!!!!!!!!!!!!!!!!!!!!!!!!!!!!!!!!!!!!
```

Each file is checked (and reported) twice because we are using hash => "best", which according to the documentation "correlates the best two available algorithms known in the OpenSSL library." We could specify a specific algorithm (e.g. "sha256") to check each file only once.

As written, the detect_all_change body will automatically update the hashes database whenever a change is detected, but changing the value of update_hashes to "no" would prevent this from happening, and it would keep warning you about changes until you update the database.

More useful in many cases would be the ability to monitor whole directories for un-authorized changes. For this we use the same detect_all_change body, but we add additional attributes to the files: promise that uses it, so that it recurses into the directories we specify:

```
bundle agent monitor_for_changes
{
  vars:
      "files_dirs" slist => { "/bin", "/etc/passwd", "/etc/motd" };

  files:
      "$(files_dirs)"
        changes => detect_all_change,
        depth_search => recurse("inf");
}
```

Note that we are combining in the same list both directories and files that we want to monitor. When running this bundle for the first time, you will see how CFEngine populates its database of hashes:

```
# cf-agent -KI -f ./monitor_for_changes.cf
 !! File /bin/[ was not in md5 database - new file found
I: Report relates to a promise with handle ""
I: Made in version 'not specified' of './monitor_for_changes.cf' near line 14
 !! File /bin/[ was not in sha1 database - new file found
I: Report relates to a promise with handle ""
I: Made in version 'not specified' of './monitor_for_changes.cf' near line 14
 !! File /bin/bash was not in md5 database - new file found
I: Report relates to a promise with handle ""
I: Made in version 'not specified' of './monitor_for_changes.cf' near line 14
 !! File /bin/bash was not in sha1 database - new file found
I: Report relates to a promise with handle ""
I: Made in version 'not specified' of './monitor_for_changes.cf' near line 14
 !! File /bin/cat was not in md5 database - new file found
 . . .
 !! File /etc/passwd was not in sha1 database - new file found
I: Report relates to a promise with handle ""
I: Made in version 'not specified' of './monitor_for_changes.cf' near line 14
Warning: depth_search (recursion) is promised for a base object /etc/passwd
    that is not a directory
 !! File /etc/motd was not in md5 database - new file found
I: Report relates to a promise with handle ""
I: Made in version 'not specified' of './monitor_for_changes.cf' near line 14
 !! File /etc/motd was not in sha1 database - new file found
I: Report relates to a promise with handle ""
I: Made in version 'not specified' of './monitor_for_changes.cf' near line 14
Warning: depth_search (recursion) is promised for a base object /etc/motd
    that is not a directory
```

Note the two warning messages I have highlighted — CFEngines tells us that it cannot recurse into files. It will still compute the hashes and monitor the files for changes, but if we want to eliminate these spurious warnings, we can change the bundle to use two lists, one for directories and one for files:

```
bundle agent monitor_for_changes
{
  vars:
      "dirs"  slist => { "/bin/", "/usr/bin/" };
      "files" slist => { "/etc/passwd", "/etc/motd" };
```

```
files:
    "$(dirs)"
      changes => detect_all_change,
      depth_search => recurse("inf");

    "$(files)"
      changes => detect_all_change;
}
```

When using a recursive search, CFEngine will detect new and deleted files, in addition to file changes:

```
# sudo touch /bin/blah
# cf-agent -KI -f ./monitor_for_changes.cf
 !! File /bin/blah was not in md5 database - new file found
I: Report relates to a promise with handle ""
I: Made in version 'not specified' of './monitor_for_changes.cf' near line 14
 !! File /bin/blah was not in sha1 database - new file found
I: Report relates to a promise with handle ""
I: Made in version 'not specified' of './monitor_for_changes.cf' near line 14
# cf-agent -KI -f ./monitor_for_changes.cf
# sudo rm /bin/blah
# cf-agent -KI -f ./monitor_for_changes.cf
ALERT: /bin/blah file no longer exists!
I: Report relates to a promise with handle ""
I: Made in version 'not specified' of './monitor_for_changes.cf' near line 14
ALERT: /bin/blah file no longer exists!
I: Report relates to a promise with handle ""
I: Made in version 'not specified' of './monitor_for_changes.cf' near line 14
```

The weak point of any file-change monitoring solution such as the one described above, or in Tripwire, is the hashes database. If an attacker manages to modify the database, he can update it with the new hash values of any files he modifies, and those changes will not be detected nor reported.

One way in which CFEngine can help to solve this problem is by performing distributed monitoring of the hash database. CFEngine is able to automatically and transparently distribute the monitoring among groups of hosts so that if the hash database is modified in any one of them, a group of others will detect the change and notify about it. The idea is that an attacker might modify the database in a single host, but if that database is replicated across several other hosts, it's very unlikely that the attacker will be able to modify all those copies simultaneously.

For this, we again use CFEngine's file-comparison abilities, coupled with its ability to automatically determine groups of hosts. The peers() function allows us to break a list of hosts into subsets of arbitrary size, and allows each host to determine its "neighbors" in the group. Using this capability, we can instruct hosts to cross-copy the database file among themselves. For example:

```
bundle agent neighborhood_watch
{
  vars:
      "neighbors" slist => peers("/var/cfengine/inputs/hostlist","#.*",4),   ❶
```

```
        comment => "Get my neighbors from a list of all hosts";
   files:
      "$(sys.workdir)/nw/$(neighbors)_checksum_digests.db"   ❷
         comment => "Watch our peers remote hash tables!",
         copy_from => remote_cp("$(sys.workdir)/checksum_digests.db",
                                "$(neighbors)"),   ❸
         action => neighbor_report("File changes observed on $(neighbors)"),   ❹
         depends_on => { "grant_hash_tables" };   ❺
}

body action neighbor_report(msg)
{
        ifelapsed => "30";
        log_string => "$(msg)";
}
```

Let's examine how this works.

❶ We assume each client has a list of all hosts in the network stored at */var/cfengine/ inputs/hostlist*. This file could be generated by the policy hub from its "last seen" report and then copied using CFEngine to all other hosts. The peers() function splits this list into chunks of the given size (4 hosts per group in this case), and assigns into the @(neighbors) list the list of the peers of the current host. In each host, peers() will determine the group to which the current host belongs, and then return all the hosts in that group, except the current one.

❷ The files: promise will repeat for each one of the neighbors using implicit looping, and will copy their hash database into a local file under */var/cfengine/nw/*, named after the corresponding host name.

❸ The file to be copied from each neighbor is */var/cfengine/checksum_digests.db*. (This filename may change depending on the database engine that CFEngine is using. For example it would be */var/cfengine/checksum_digests.tcdb* if you are using Tokyo Cabinet.)

❹ We determine that the action to be taken when the promise is repaired is to generate a log message about it, indicating the host in which the discrepancy was found.

Let's analyze for a moment the behavior of this code. It's a simple file-copy operation, like the ones we use to copy updated policies from the policy hub into the clients. However, in this case we are dealing with a file that should very rarely change, so whenever it changes, it's a noteworthy event. When the hash database is modified in any of the neighbors, the other neighbors will notice this change and re-copy the file to their local disk. The promise is marked as repaired, and a message is generated.

❺ The correct execution of this neighborhood-watch technique depends on being able to copy the hash databases among neighbors. For this reason, we make this promise dependent on another promise that sets the appropriate access rules for the file, and which must be defined in a bundle of type server:

```
bundle server access_rules()
{
```

```
vars:
    # List here the IP masks that we grant access to on the server
    "acl" slist => {
                     "$(sys.ipv4)/24",
                     "128.39.89.233",
                     "2001:700:700:3.*"
                   },
        comment => "Define an acl for the machines to be granted accesses",
        handle => "common_def_vars_acl";

access:
    "/var/cfengine/checksum_digests.tcdb"
        handle  => "grant_hash_tables",
        admit   => { @(acl) },
        maproot => { @(acl) };
}
```

Bundles of this type define behavior of the `cf-serverd` process, and among other things, define which machines can access which files through it. The `cf-serverd` process running on each machine is the one that will provide access to the */var/cfengine/checksum_digests.db* file so that neighbors can copy it as described before. For this to work, we are using an `access:` promise to specify who can read this file. The `admit` attribute indicates which IP addresses will have permission to access the file, and the `maproot` attribute indicates which machines can have access to any file on the system. We set both of these attributes to the value of the `@(acl)` list, which we define in the `vars:` section. The first value in `@(acl)` is `"$(sys.ipv4)/24"`, which indicates that we want the whole class-C network segment (`/24`) in which the machine is located (`$(sys.ipv4)` contains the current IP address), to have access[3]. We also specify, for the sake of example, two individual IP addresses (one IPv4, one IPv6) as part of `@(acl)`.

Using this technique, we can have a self-maintaining, self-protecting system for monitoring file changes. We can add more hosts into the peer groups to increase security, (by increasing the number from 4 to whatever we need), at the expense of additional file copy operations among the hosts.

---

3. This is just an example. You would of course need to adapt it according to the specifics of your network.

## CHAPTER 5

CFEngine Tips, Tricks, and Patterns

In previous chapters we have seen a number of CFEngine policies to achieve different specific tasks, with the intention of introducing you to a number of basic CFEngine concepts. Now that you know those basic concepts, I would like to introduce you to several generic techniques and patterns that are generally useful when writing CFEngine policies. Mastering these techniques will help you write more concise and efficient CFEngine code.

Hierarchical Copying

One of the common uses of CFEngine is to copy files (configuration files, binaries, libraries, documentation, etc.) into systems. If you maintain a heterogeneous network consisting of different system types, operating systems, architectures, and applications, you will at some point need to copy different sets of files onto different systems. The most straightforward way of achieving this would be to have different promises in your files: section for different hard classes that reflect the different system categories you want to differentiate. For example, you may want to copy different */etc/hosts* files depending on operating system:

```
files:
  ubuntu_10::
    "/etc/hosts"
      copy_from => mycopy("$(repository)/etc.hosts.ubuntu_10");
  suse_9::
    "/etc/hosts"
      copy_from => mycopy("$(repository)/etc.hosts.suse_9");
  redhat_5::
    "/etc/hosts"
      copy_from => mycopy("$(repository)/etc.hosts.redhat_5");
```

This example can be easily simplified if you know that the built-in CFEngine variable $(sys.flavor) contains the type and version of the operating system, so we could rewrite this example as follows:

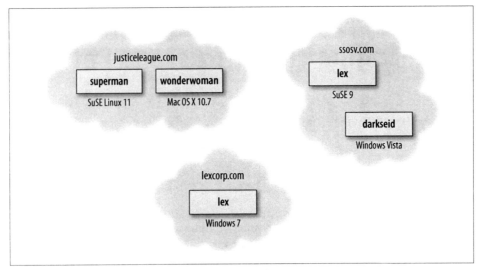

Figure 5-1. Sample network with multiple domains and operating systems

```
"/etc/hosts"
    copy_from => mycopy("$(repository)/etc.$(sys.flavor)");
```

You could use any variable, whether defined by you or pre-defined by CFEngine, for a rule like this. All the built-in variables are documented in the CFEngine Reference Guide (*https://cfengine.com/manuals/cf3-reference#Special-Variables*).

However, this method suffers from several drawbacks:

- You need to have a separate file for every possible value of the variable you are using ($(sys.flavor) in this case). For example, if you have hosts that are running SuSE 10, SuSE 11 and Ubuntu 10, you will need to have the files *hosts.suse_10*, *hosts.suse_11* and *hosts.ubuntu_10* in the repository, even if they are all the same. There is no easy way to implement a "catch all" clause for copying a generic file.

- You are restricted to using a single variable to differentiate among systems. If you want some files to be different according to architecture, or domain name, or any other information, you need to write separate promises.

What we would like to do is to implement the copy operation according to arbitrary criteria, as contained in CFEngine classes and variables. For example, consider the network shown in Figure 5-1. We would like to copy different versions of the */etc/ hosts* file to different hosts, according to criteria such as their hostname, their domain name, their type of operating system (Windows, Linux, etc.) and their specific OS "flavor" (e.g. SuSE 9, RedHat 5, etc.). It's worth noting that all of these attributes are discovered automatically by CFEngine and stored both in variables and in hard classes. For example, in a SuSE 9 system the classes linux, suse, suse_9 will be defined, and the variables $(sys.class) and $(sys.flavor) will contain "linux" and "suse_9", respectively.

For the sake of this example, let's assume that *$(repository)/etc/* contains the following files (listed in alphabetical order):

```
hosts
hosts.justiceleague.com
hosts.lex
hosts.ssosv.com
hosts.suse_9
hosts.windows
hosts.wonderwoman.justiceleague.com
```

Using this information, we can hardcode these rules in promises like these:

```
body agent control
{
    # Single copy for all files
    files_single_copy => { ".*" }; ❶
}

bundle agent test
{
  files: ❷
    wonderwoman_justiceleague_com::
      "/etc/hosts"
       copy_from => local_cp("$(repository)/etc/hosts.wonderwoman.justiceleague.com");
    lex::
      "/etc/hosts"
        copy_from => local_cp("$(repository)/etc/hosts.lex");
    justiceleague_com::
      "/etc/hosts"
        copy_from => local_cp("$(repository)/etc/hosts.justiceleague.com");
    ssosv_com::
      "/etc/hosts"
        copy_from => local_cp("$(repository)/etc/hosts.ssosv.com");
    suse_9::
      "/etc/hosts"
        copy_from => local_cp("$(repository)/etc/hosts.suse_9");
    windows::
      "/etc/hosts"
        copy_from => local_cp("$(repository)/etc/hosts.windows");
    any::
      "/etc/hosts"
        copy_from => local_cp("$(repository)/etc/hosts");
}
```

Assuming the $(repository) variable has been set elsewhere, this works as follows:

❶ First, we have to enable "single copy" on all the files we want to process. This is a configuration parameter that tells CFEngine to copy each file at most once, ignoring successive copy operations for the same destination file. The files_single_copy parameter in the **agent** control body specifies a list of regular expressions to match filenames to which single-copy should apply. By setting it to ".*" we match all filenames. You could customize this to apply it only to certain files, although in my opinion this would tend to complicate understanding of the promises by having different copy behavior for different files.

❷ In the `files:` promise section, we list multiple file-copy promises conditioned by each one of the classes with which we want to differentiate the hosts. Again, remember that all of these classes (`wonderwoman_justiceleague_com`, `lex`, `justicelea gue_com`, `suse_9`, etc.) are hard classes that will be automatically set by CFEngine on systems with the corresponding characteristics. We have listed the classes from most specific to more general (with the `any` class expression at the end, which will catch anything that is not matched by the previous sections). CFEngine will process these promises in the order they appear. The first one to match (this is, for which the corresponding class is defined in the current host) will execute, resulting in the copy operation from the appropriate file in the repository. More general classes may match, but because of the `files_single_copy` parameter, they will be ignored after the file is copied for the first time.

This works, but suffers from many of the same problems we saw before: it is verbose and the class names and filenames are hard-coded in the policy.

A more flexible way to achieve this task is known in CFEngine terminology as "hierarchical copy." In this pattern, you specify an arbitrary list of variables by which you want files to be differentiated, and the order in which they should be considered, from most specific to most general. When the copy promise is executed, the most specific file found will be copied.

This pattern is very simple to implement:

```
body agent control
{
        files_single_copy => { ".*" };
}

bundle agent test
{
  vars:
      "suffixes"   slist => { ".$(sys.fqhost)", ".$(sys.uqhost)", ".$(sys.domain)",
                              ".$(sys.flavor)", ".$(sys.ostype)", "" };
  files:
      "/etc/hosts"
        copy_from => local_cp("$(repository)/etc/hosts$(suffixes)");
}
```

As you can see, we are defining a list variable called @(suffixes) that contains the criteria by which we want to differentiate the files. All the variables contained in the list are automatically defined by CFEngine, and correspond to the classes we used in the previous example. Then we simply include that variable, as a scalar, in our `copy_from` parameter. Because CFEngine does automatic list expansion, it will try each variable in turn, executing the copy promise multiple times (one for each value in the list) and copy the first file that exists. For example, in our Linux SuSE 11 machine called superman.justiceleague.com, the @(suffixes) variable will contain the following values:

```
{ ".superman.justiceleague.com", ".superman", ".justiceleague.com", ".suse_11",
  ".linux", "" }
```

When the file-copy promise is executed, implicit looping will cause these strings to be appended in sequence to "$(repository)/etc/hosts", so the following filenames will be attempted in sequence: *hosts.superman.justiceleague.com*, *hosts.justiceleague.com*, *hosts.suse_11*, *hosts.linux* and *hosts*. The first one to exist (in this case, *hosts.justiceleague.com*) will be copied over */etc/hosts* in the client, and the rest will be skipped. Of course, for this to work, we also need to set the files_single_copy parameter as described before.

Now, for our host darkseid.ssosv.com, which is a Windows machine, the list will contain the following values:

```
{ ".darkseid.ssosv.com", ".darkseid", ".ssosv.com", ".windows_7", ".windows", "" }
```

All the values will be attempted until *hosts.windows* is found and copied over.

Wonder Woman needs a specific hosts file for her machine (perhaps so that she can reach certain hosts in Paradise Island), and so she gets *hosts.wonderwoman.justiceleague.com*, the first try on the list. Similarly, the lists for Lex Luthor's machines look like this:

For lex.ssosv.com:
```
{ ".lex.ssosv.com", ".lex", ".ssosv.com", ".suse_9", ".linux", "" }
```
For lex.lexcorp.com:
```
{ ".lex.lexcorp.com", ".lex", ".lexcorp.com", ".windows_7", ".windows", "" }
```

Therefore, both machines get the same file (*hosts.lex*) because that is the first one that exists when going through the lists.

For hosts that don't match any of the existing files, the last item on the list (an empty string) will cause the generic *hosts* file to be copied. Note that the dot for each of the filenames is included in $(suffixes), except for the last element.

As you can see, this allows us to have different files copied according to arbitrary criteria. Using this technique, you can drastically reduce the number of file-copying promises in your policy, while still having a lot of flexibility in which files are copied.

 This technique, by its very nature, frequently tries to copy non-existent files (until it finds one that exists, and stops there). This results in messages from *cf-agent* about the files it cannot find. You may see messages like these as the different possibilities are attempted:

```
Can't stat /var/cfengine/masterfiles/files/etc/hosts.darkseid.ssosv.com
  in files.copyfrom promise
Can't stat /var/cfengine/masterfiles/files/etc/hosts.darkseid
  in files.copyfrom promise
Can't stat /var/cfengine/masterfiles/files/etc/hosts.ssosv.com
  in files.copyfrom promise
```

```
Can't stat /var/cfengine/masterfiles/files/etc/hosts.windows_7
    in files.copyfrom promise
    -> Copying from 10.6.5.4:/var/cfengine/masterfiles/files/etc/hosts.windows
```

This can result in noisy logs, but these messages can, of course, be safely
ignored.

Now let's put this pattern in a more complex example. We will put the files and directories to copy in lists, so that we can apply implicit looping on them as well, and add
a few more bells and whistles:

```
body agent control
{
        files_single_copy => { ".*" };  ❶
}

bundle agent copyfiles
{
  vars:
        # Suffixes to try, in most-specific to most-general order. This must include the
        # empty suffix at the end, for the most general file.
        "suffixes"    slist => { ".$(sys.fqhost)", ".$(sys.uqhost)", ".$(sys.domain)",  ❷
                                 ".$(sys.flavor)", ".$(sys.ostype)", "" };
        # List of files to copy
        "filestocopy"    slist => { "/etc/hosts", "/etc/motd" };   ❸
        "dirstocopy"     slist => { "$(sys.workdir)/bin", "/usr/local/bin" };
        # Source of the files
        "repo"           string => "/mnt/fileserver/cfengine/files";   ❹
        # Destination for the files
        # Set this to an empty string for a production environment
        # "dest" string => "";
        "dest"           string => "/tmp/testdest";   ❺

  files:
        "$(dest)$(filestocopy)"   ❻
          copy_from => local_dcp("$(repo)$(filestocopy)$(suffixes)");

        "$(dest)$(dirstocopy)"   ❼
          copy_from => local_dcp("$(repo)$(dirstocopy)$(suffixes)"),
          depth_search => recurse("inf");
}
```

This is how it works:

❶ As before, we set the `files_single_copy` parameter to ensure each file is copied at
most once.

❷ We store in `@(suffixes)` the list of file suffixes to try. Just as before, we will be
selecting the most-specific file according to fully-qualified host name
(`$(sys.fqhost)`), plain host name (`$(sys.uqhost)`), domain name (`$(sys.domain)`),
operating system name and version (`$(sys.flavor)`) and top-level operating system
type (`$(sys.ostype)`). Finally, the empty element will select the generic file (without
any suffix) to be copied.

---

❸ We store in @(filestocopy) the list of individual files to copy from the repository, and in @(dirstocopy) the list of directories to copy. From the point of view of CFEngine syntax, files and directories could be in the same list, but there is an important semantic difference: When a full directory is copied, the suffix is expected to appear in the directory name (for example, */usr/local/bin.suse_9* or */usr/local/bin.windows*), and the selected directory will be copied in its entirety, without any further filtering on the files it contains. This is useful for directories among which there exist no common files (as may be the case for directories containing executable files).

❹ We store in $(repo) the top-level source location for the files. In this example, all files are being copied locally. Depending on your implementation details, you may need to define a source host as well, and modify the copy_from attributes to use CFEngine's remote-file-copy capabilities.

❺ We store in $(dest) the top-level destination for the files. In this case, for testing purposes, all the files wil be copied under */tmp/testdest*. In production, most likely this variable would be empty, so that files are copied to their real locations.

❻ We finally get to the file-copy promises. The first one takes care of copying individual files. We are using the standard library's local_dcp() definition, which does a local copy using a cryptographic hash as the comparison, and receives the source file name as its only argument:

```
body copy_from local_dcp(from)
{
        source      => "$(from)";
        compare     => "digest";
}
```

In this promise, the destination file is specified as "$(dest)$(filestocopy)", which means that implicit looping will happen over the contents of the @(filestocopy) list, and each one will be prepended with the destination directory. For example, when $(filestocopy) has the value "/etc/hosts", the destination file will be "/tmp/testd est/etc/hosts". When the policy goes in production and we modify $(dest) to be an empty string, the destination file will be simply "/etc/hosts".

The source file (the argument to local_dcp()) is a bit more complicated. In this case we are doing implicit looping over two lists: @(filestocopy) and @(suffixes), and the file-copy promise will be evaluated repeatedly for each combination. For example, if @(suffixes) contains the following values:

```
{ ".lex.lexcorp.com", ".lex", ".lexcorp.com", ".windows_7", ".windows", "" }
```

Then when $(filestocopy) has the value "/etc/hosts", the argument to local_dcp() will take the following values in sequence:

- "/mnt/fileserver/cfengine/files/etc/hosts.lex.lexcorp.com"
- "/mnt/fileserver/cfengine/files/etc/hosts.lex"
- "/mnt/fileserver/cfengine/files/etc/hosts.lexcorp.com"

- "/mnt/fileserver/cfengine/files/etc/hosts.windows_7"
- "/mnt/fileserver/cfengine/files/etc/hosts.windows"
- "/mnt/fileserver/cfengine/files/etc/hosts"

Only the first file found will be copied to */etc/hosts*, and the rest will be skipped.

❼ The promise to copy whole directories works the same way, with the difference that it loops over the contents of @(dirstocopy), and the file-copy promise is given the additional attribute `depth_search`, with an argument that indicates a recursive copy should be done (`recurse()` is also defined in the standard library). As I mentioned before, we could even merge these two promises, since `depth_search` is simply ignored for plain files, but I like having the conceptual distinction between them.

CFEngine keeps track of already-copied files only at the individual file level and not at the directory level. If one of the less-specific directories contains files that do not exist in a more-specific directory, they will be copied as well, even if the more-specific directory gets copied too. For example, if *$(repo)/usr/local/bin/* contains a file called *latex* and this file does not exist in *$(repo)/usr/local/bin.lex.lexcorp.com/*, it will be copied to the destination */usr/local/bin/*, because that specific file is not flagged as "already copied" by CFEngine. This can lead to unexpected consequences, although it can also be used to reduce repetition among directories. For example, you could put all the binaries in *$(repo)/usr/local/bin.lex.lexcorp.com/*, and leave all the platform-independent shell scripts in *$(repo)/usr/local/bin/*. The resulting */usr/local/bin/* in the clients will contain the merger of both directories.

Hierarchical copy is a powerful technique that can greatly simplify the structure of your CFEngine policies. File manipulation is one of the most powerful and complex topics in CFEngine. I strongly advise you to carefully read the relevant sections of the Reference Guide, to get an idea of the multiple capabilities that CFEngine offers in this respect.

Passing Name-Value Pairs to Bundles

Many system configuration tasks require groups of name-value pairs to be associated with a single entity. Some of these tasks include:

- Editing configuration files in which parameters and their values need to be stored. The pairs may be further associated with a single portion of the file identified by a name (for example, Windows-style INI files contain parameters grouped in named sections).

- Setting user parameters. In this case, sets of pairs are associated with a single user, identified by name.

This is a technique that you have seen used many times in this book. The name-value pairs are stored in a CFEngine array, with the parameter names used as indices, and with the values stored in each element of the array. For example, for configuring */etc/ssh/sshd_config* and */etc/sysctl.conf* in "Initial System Configuration" on page 69, we defined two arrays (named sshd and sysctl) in the configfiles() bundle. We also used an array to store the filenames of the files we were going to edit::

```
bundle agent configfiles
{
  vars:
      # Files to edit
      "files[sysctl]" string => "/etc/sysctl.conf";
      "files[sshd]"   string => "/etc/ssh/sshd_config";

      # Sysctl variables to set
      "sysctl[net.ipv4.tcp_syncookies]"               string => "1";
      "sysctl[net.ipv4.conf.all.accept_source_route]" string => "0";
      "sysctl[net.ipv4.conf.all.accept_redirects]"    string => "0";
      "sysctl[net.ipv4.conf.all.rp_filter]"           string => "1";
      "sysctl[net.ipv4.conf.all.log_martians]"        string => "1";

      # SSHD configuration to set
      "sshd[Protocol]"                                string => "2";
      "sshd[X11Forwarding]"                           string => "yes";
      "sshd[UseDNS]"                                  string => "no";

  methods:
      "sysctl"  usebundle => edit_sysctl;
      "sshd"    usebundle => edit_sshd;
}
```

Having sets of related values in a single array has a number of advantages, since they can be manipulated by a single set of promises just by varying the indices used to access them. To make use of this array, you have to pass it as an argument to a bundle. One of the most useful functions in this technique is getindices(), which returns a list containing the indices of the given array, and can be used to produce an enumeration of the elements over which to iterate (the complementary function to get just the values is getvalues()). For example, remember from the edit_sshd() bundle:

```
files:
    "$(configfiles.files[sshd])"
      handle => "edit_sshd",
      comment => "Set desired sshd_config parameters",
      edit_line => set_config_values("configfiles.sshd"),
      classes => if_repaired("restart_sshd");
```

To pass arrays as arguments we must pass a string with the name of the array, and then dereference it inside the function (in this case, the dereferencing is happening in the set_config_values() bundle). The argument we are passing to set_config_values() is "configfiles.sshd", which refers to the sshd array defined in the configfiles() bundle.

To group name/value sets into named groups, we can use two-dimensional arrays, as we saw in the `create_users()` bundle in "User Management" on page 91:

```
bundle agent manage_users
{
  vars:
      "users[root][fullname]"    string => "System administrator";
      "users[root][uid]"         string => "0";
      "users[root][gid]"         string => "0";
      "users[root][home]"        string => "/root";
      "users[root][shell]"       string => "/bin/bash";
      "users[root][flags]"       string => "-o -m";
      "users[root][password]"    string => "FkDMzhB1WnOp2";
      "users[zamboni][fullname]" string => "Diego Zamboni";
      "users[zamboni][uid]"      string => "501";
      "users[zamboni][gid]"      string => "users";
      "users[zamboni][home]"     string => "/home/zamboni";
      "users[zamboni][shell]"    string => "/bin/bash";
      "users[zamboni][flags]"    string => "-m";
      "users[zamboni][password]" string => "dk52ia209rfuh";
  methods:
      "users"    usebundle => create_users("manage_users.users");
}
```

In this case the dereferencing can get a little complicated. For example, let us look at some of the code inside the `create_users()` bundle:

```
bundle agent create_users(info)
{
  vars:
      "user"        slist => getindices("$(info)");

  classes:
      "add_$(user)" not => userexists("$(user)");

  commands:
    linux::
      "/usr/sbin/useradd $($(info)[$(user)][flags]) -u $($(info)[$(user)][uid])
       -g $($(info)[$(user)][gid]) -d $($(info)[$(user)][home])
       -s $($(info)[$(user)][shell]) -c '$($(info)[$(user)][fullname])' $(user)"
       ifvarclass => "add_$(user)";
  ...
```

This bundle is being called from the `methods:` section of the `manage_users()` bundle, with the string `"manage_users.users"` as the value of `$(info)`. We use `getindices()` directly on this value to get a list of the first-level indices of the array (the user names), which we store in `@(user)`. Then we use implicit looping over `@(user)` to cycle through all those values, and we use the following construction to access individual elements of each user's data: `$($(info)[$(user)][field])`. This expands to `$(manage_users.users[$(user)][field])`, on which implicit looping is applied through the `$(user)` variable. Remember that parenthesis (or curly braces, they mean the same) are required around the whole expression, so that CFEngine recognizes it properly as a variable reference.

While the syntax can be complicated, this data structure allows great flexibility in passing around and using data structures to be used in configuration operations.

You can see this pattern used in many places, not only in the examples we have described in this book, but also in the standard library, for example in the set_config_values(), set_variable_values(), and append_users_starting() bundles.

Setting Default Values for Bundle Parameters

One potential issue, particularly with complex bundles that may have many different options, is the need to provide default parameter values. These may be overridden by the user, but let you avoid having to specify all those values in every single call. Happily, this is also possible with CFEngine when you pass parameters in an array, as described in the previous section.

The trick is to set the default values in an array internal to the bundle, and then copy the parameters passed in as arguments on top of that array. When no value is passed for a particular parameter, its old value (the default) will be retained. We saw an example of this technique in the wp_vars() bundle in "Manual Software Management" on page 99:

```
bundle agent wp_vars(params)    ❶
{
  vars:
      "wp_dir"                string => "$($(params)[_wp_dir])";
      # Default configuration values. Internal parameters start with _
      "conf[_tarfile]"        string => "/root/wordpress-latest.tar.gz",    ❷
        policy => "overridable";    ❸
      "conf[_downloadurl]"    string => "http://wordpress.org/latest.tar.gz",
        policy => "overridable";
      "conf[_wp_config]"      string => "$(wp_dir)/wp-config.php",
        policy => "overridable";
      "conf[_wp_cfgsample]" string => "$(wp_dir)/wp-config-sample.php",
        policy => "overridable";
    debian::    ❹
      "conf[_sys_servicecmd]" string => "/usr/sbin/service",
        policy => "overridable";
      "conf[_sys_apachesrv]"  string => "apache2",
        policy => "overridable";
    redhat::
      "conf[_sys_servicecmd]" string => "/sbin/service",
        policy => "overridable";
      "conf[_sys_apachesrv]"  string => "httpd",
        policy => "overridable";
    any::    ❺
      # Copy configuration parameters passed, into a local array
      "param_keys"            slist  => getindices("$(params)");    ❻
      "conf[$(param_keys)]" string => "$($(params)[$(param_keys)])",
        policy => "overridable";
}
```

❶ The bundle receives the name of an array as its $(params) argument.

❷ Default values for all parameters are stored in an internal array called conf. Here we are storing the default values for parameters _tarfile, _downloadurl, _wp_config and _wp_cfgsample[1].

❸ Note that all the array elements are assigned with their policy attribute set to "overridable", which means that they can be assigned a new value later on. By default, all variables in CFEngine are immutable, and you will get an error if you try to reassign a value to them. This policy setting changes this behavior, allowing them to be freely redefined.

❹ We set some of the parameters in sections conditioned to certain classes. In this case, we have certain parameters that have different values on Debian-based systems and on RedHat-based systems. Note that these are also stored with policy set to "overridable", so that they can be redefined by the user.

❺ We condition the final section to the any class, so that the following statements are again executed for all systems. Note that this any:: block must come last, since promises within a single section (vars: in this case) are executed in the order they appear in the file.

❻ And finally, we come to copying the user-provided parameters on top of the conf array. For this, we first store all the indices from $(params) into a list, and then, using implicit looping, copy all those elements from the $(params) array onto conf. Again, we set policy to "overridable" so that the copy can be done without any warnings. Any parameters passed in the $(params) array will overwrite the previous values in the conf array. After this, the $(params) array becomes unnecessary, and the rest of the bundle should access any values it needs from the conf array.

This technique is generally applicable, and adds the convenience of only having to specify those parameters that deviate from the standard, when using a bundle.

Implicit looping, combined with arrays, and with the ability to specify default parameter values, provide a powerful mechanism that allows us to pass around data and perform elaborate tasks without any flow-control code at all.

Using Classes as Configuration Mechanisms

Classes are the universal decision-taking mechanism in CFEngine, and we have seen already throughout the book many examples of using classes, either automatically discovered or set programatically, to control the behavior of CFEngine policies. I would like to draw your attention now to the use of classes as a manual configuration and

---

1. All the parameter names shown in this example start with an underscore, but this has no implicit meaning. It's just a convention used in the Wordpress installer to indicate internal parameters that will not be written to the WordPress configuration file.

control mechanism. Due to their Boolean nature, certain classes can be used throughout the entire policy to enforce certain desired behaviors.

We saw a simple example of this in "Editing /etc/sysctl.conf" on page 69:

```
commands:
  sysctl_modified.!no_restarts::
    "/sbin/sysctl -p"
      handle => "reload_sysctl",
      comment => "Make sure new sysctl settings are loaded";
```

Here, the no_restarts class is being used as a flag to control whether the command to reload the *sysctl* settings should be executed. Normally this is desirable so that the changes take effect immediately, but under certain circumstances (for example when testing, or when making a large number of changes) we may want to disable this behavior. By defining the no_restarts class, the whole class expression becomes false, and the command will not be executed. By using a construct like this consistently throughout a policy, we can control this behavior with a single class definition.

There are several ways in which a class like this can be defined. It could be defined in a common bundle, so that it becomes a global class, evaluated very early in the processing of the policy and so assured to have the desired effect:

```
bundle common g
{
  classes:
    "no_restarts" expression => "!any";
}
```

This code makes the class undefined (false) by default ("any" is the CFEngine equivalent of an always-true expression, so negating it results in an always-false expression; completely omitting the class definition would have the same effect). To change this, we would need to simply remove the exclamation mark from the class expression. To modify the class during a single run of *cf-agent*, we could specify it in the command line using the -D option. Any classes defined through this mechanism override definitions found in the policy, so without modifying the policy file, we could run it with -Dno_restarts and have it defined for that run only.

If we want to avoid having to modify the policy files and also having to specify options in the command line, we could specify the class in a text file that is distributed to each machine, and from where class definitions are read. We would replace our common bundle with something like this:

```
bundle common g
{
  vars:
    "class_file" string => "/var/cfengine/site/classes.txt";
    "class_strs" slist => readstringlist("$(class_file)",
                                         "#.*$", "\s+", "inf", "inf");
  classes:
    "$(class_strs)" expression => "any";
}
```

In this case, we are defining a file from which class definitions will be read, and then reading that file into a list of strings called @(class_strs) using the readstringlist() function. Its arguments specify the file to read, the regular expression pattern to use as comments (in this case, a hash sign followed by an arbitrary string until the end of the line), the list element separator (we are using "\s+", so that multiple space-separated elements can be included in the same line), and the maximum number of lines and bytes to read (both set to "inf" to read as many as we can). In the classes: section, we are looping over that list, defining classes named after each one of those elements. Thus, if we want to define the no_restarts classes, all we need to do is add to the /var/cfengine/ site/classes.txt file a line that contains the string "no_restarts".

This mechanism offers great flexibility because the classes.txt file can be set by hand, created at system install time according to its characteristics, or modified by CFEngine itself—for example, using templates or hierarchical copying—to contain different values according to any criteria we want to define.

The abortclasses attribute of body agent control can be used to define classes that should cause CFEngine to stop execution immediately. For example, you could define a class that, if defined, will disable CFEngine in the current host:

```
body agent control
{
        abortclasses => { "disable_cfengine" };
}
```

If you have this attribute defined, the classes.txt file is an ideal place for specifying the disable_cfengine class if it becomes necessary to disable CFEngine for any reason. If you are distributing classes.txt using hierarchical copying as described in "Hierarchical Copying" on page 119, you can make this change as specific or broad as you wish.

In fact, we can combine these mechanisms in the same policy. For example, while writing this code I used a policy like this to make testing easier by passing the -Dtestrun flag to control the value of $(class_file):

```
bundle common g
{
  vars:
    testrun::
      "class_file" string => "/tmp/classes.txt";
    !testrun::
      "class_file" string => "/var/cfengine/site/classes.txt";
    any::
      "class_strs" slist => readstringlist("$(class_file)",
                                           "#.*?\n", "\s+", "inf", "inf");
  classes:
      "$(class_strs)"  expression => "any";
}
```

Generic Tasks Using Lists and Array Indices

Implicit looping over lists and array indices can be used as a building block for concise and reusable policies (sometimes at the expense of readability of the lower-level blocks, which need to do a lot of variable dereferencing).

The general pattern of this technique when using arrays is the following:

```
vars:
  "array[id1]"    string => "value1";
  "array[id2]"    string => "value2";
...
# (possibly in a different bundle)
  "index"         slist => getindices("array");
...
# Use $(index) in promises to make them loop over all the IDs
# and do something with their values
```

One example of this technique is to use the @(files) array we defined with the names of the files to edit, as a mechanism to automatically back up files before making any changes in the configfiles() bundle we defined throughout Chapter 4:

```
bundle agent configfiles
{
  vars:
      # Files to edit
      "files[sysctl]" string => "/etc/sysctl.conf";
      "files[sshd]" string => "/etc/ssh/sshd_config";
      "files[inittab]"    string => "/etc/inittab";
      ...

  methods:
      # Pass the name of the array, not the array itself.
      "backup"  usebundle => backup_files("configfiles.files");
      "sysctl"  usebundle => edit_sysctl;
      "sshd"    usebundle => edit_sshd;
      "inittab" usebundle => edit_inittab;
      "users"   usebundle => manage_users("configfiles.users");
}

bundle agent backup_files(id)
{
  vars:
      "allfiles" slist => getindices("$(id)");

  files:
      "$(allfiles).original"
        comment => "Ensure we have a backup of previous versions of $(allfiles)",
        copy_from => backup_local_cp("$(allfiles)");
}
```

Here we have inserted a call to backup_files() before all the other bundle calls, with the name of the @(configfiles.files) array as an argument. This bundle uses implicit looping over all the elements of the array, copying each file onto a backup file with ".original" as a suffix.

You might ask at this point: why not just use CFEngine's built-in backup behavior, which can be defined in an `edit_defaults` body part, as we saw in "Editing /etc/init-tab" on page 83? The technique shown in this section does not preclude the use of `edit_defaults` specification, but there are several advantages to doing this as well:

- The backup step becomes explicit and centralized (all the backups are done by a single bundle), which helps to make the intention of the policy clearer.
- The backup will protect against any changes made to the files, not only those made by file-editing promises (for example, changes made by copying files from a remote location, or by external commands invoked by CFEngine).
- We have more flexibility as to where and how the backup is done. For example, we could decide to have timestamped directories for all the files, kept on a remote file server. To do this, we could replace `backup_files()` with something like this:

```
bundle agent backup_files(id)
{
  vars:
      "allfiles"  slist => getindices("$(id)");
      "backupdst" string => "/mnt/fileserver/cfenginebackups-$(sys.cdate)";

  files:
      "$(backupst)/."
        create => "true";

      "$(backupdst)/$(allfiles)"
        comment => "Ensure we have a backup of previous versions of $(allfiles)",
        copy_from => local_cp("$(allfiles)");
}
```

Now we are specifying in `$(backupdst)` the destination directory where the backup files will be placed, named with a current timestamp. In the `files:` section, the first promise makes sure the destination directory exists, and the second one copies the files into it by looping over the `$(allfiles)` list.

We could go even further and use the indices of an array to determine the sequence of bundles to call in a complex policy. For example, our `configfiles()` bundle from before could be rewritten like this:

```
bundle agent configfiles
{
  vars:
      # Files to edit
      "files[sysctl]"    string => "/etc/sysctl.conf";
      "files[sshd]"      string => "/etc/ssh/sshd_config";
      "files[inittab]"   string => "/etc/inittab";
      ...

      "file_id" slist => getindices("files");
```

```
        "bundle_names" slist => maplist("edit_$(this)", "file_id");

    methods:
        "backup"   usebundle => backup_files("configfiles.files");
        "$(bundle_names)"  usebundle => $(bundle_names)("configfiles.files");
        "users"    usebundle => manage_users("configfiles.users");
}
```

Now we are defining a list called @(file_id) that contains all the indices from the files array (sysctl, sshd, etc.). Based on it, we define another list called @(method_names) that contains the names of the bundles that we want to call.

 The maplist() function that we use to convert one list into another was only introduced in CFEngine Community 3.3.0.

In the methods: section, we substitute all the calls to the file-editing bundles by a generic promise, which loops over the values of @(bundle_names) and calls the appropriate bundle by interpolating the $(bundle_names) variable into the bundle name. Note how we can also pass arguments to the bundle.

In this particular example, we are reducing the number of methods: promises from three to one, so it's not a big savings. But imagine that as your policy grows, this technique could save many lines, and more importantly, allow you to add new bundle calls simply by adding new elements to the files array, thus reducing the possibility of errors.

This type of technique can be used with any list to implement generic tasks. For example, consider this example (included in the *examples/* directory of the CFEngine source distribution):

```
bundle agent test
{
  methods:
      "Patch Group"
          comment => "Apply OS specific patches and modifications",
          usebundle => "$(sys.class)_fix";
}
```

In this case, we are using the built-in variable $(sys.class) (which contains the "class" of operating system, e.g. linux, darwin, solaris, etc.) to call a different bundle depending on the operating system of the current host. In this case, we would of course need to define bundles called linux_fix(), darwin_fix(), solaris_fix(), etc., to handle the actual calls, but the top-level intention remains clear and concise.

One final example shows how we can use nested implicit looping to implement an extensible and flexible system with very little code:

```
body common control
{
        bundlesequence => { "test" };
}
```

```
bundle agent test
{
  vars:
      "m" slist  => { "login", "ssh_keys", "environment" };
      "user" slist => { "diego", "mark", "neil" };
  methods:
      "set of $(m)" usebundle => $(m)("$(user)");
}
bundle agent login(x)
{
  reports:
    cfengine_3::
      "Setup login for $(x)";
}
bundle agent ssh_keys(x)
{
  reports:
    cfengine_3::
      "Setup ssh keys for $(x)";
}
bundle agent environment(x)
{
  reports:
    cfengine_3::
      "Setup login environment for $(x)";
}
```

In this case, we have two lists: @(m) contains the names of the bundles to call (login,
ssh_keys, environment) and @(user) contains the list of parameters to pass to the bundles. By using both variables in the methods: call, CFEngine will loop over both lists
and make the appropriate calls with the appropriate parameters in sequence:

```
$ cf-agent -KI -f ./unit_method_var2.cf
R: Setup login for diego
R: Setup ssh keys for diego
R: Setup login environment for diego
R: Setup login for mark
R: Setup ssh keys for mark
R: Setup login environment for mark
R: Setup login for neil
R: Setup ssh keys for neil
R: Setup login environment for neil
```

Defining Classes for Groups of Hosts

One of the very common patterns in CFEngine is to define classes for different groups
of hosts, and then use those classes to apply different configurations. Remember that
CFEngine automatically defines hard classes based on the hostname and the IP address
of the current host, and these classes can be tested for in class expressions.

In its simplest form, you could list individual hosts that need to be part of the class:

```
bundle agent config
{
  classes:
      "websrv"     or => { "websrv1_domain_com",
                           "websrv2_domain_com",
                           "websrv3_domain_com"
                         };
      "dnssrv"     or => { "dnssrv1_domain_com",
                           "dnssrv2_domain_com"
                         };
      ...
  methods:
    websrv::
      "config_websrv"   usebundle => config_websrv;
    dnssrv::
      "config_dnssrv"   usebundle => conig_dnssrv;
}
```

In this case, the classes websrv and dnssrv are being defined based on a boolean expression of other classes, specified by the or keyword. What this means for the dnssrv class, for example, is *"if the dnssrv1_domain_com class is defined OR the dnssrv2_comain_com class is defined, then define the dnssrv class"*. As you may remember, CFEngine automatically defines hard classes based on, among other things, the current hostname. If the current hostname is *dnssrv1.domain.com*, the dnssrv1_domain_com class will be defined (dots are not valid in class names). The end result is that the dnssrv class will be set whenever the policy is evaluated in the dnssrv1.domain.com or in the dnssrv2.domain.com hosts, and analogously for the websrv class.

However, if you have a consistent host naming scheme, you could greatly simplify this pattern by using the classmatch() function:

```
bundle agent config
{
  classes:
      "websrv"    expression => classmatch("websrv.*");
      "dnssrv"    expression => classmatch("dnssrv.*");
      ...
  methods:
    websrv::
      "config_websrv"   usebundle => config_websrv;
    dnssrv::
      "config_dnssrv"   usebundle => conig_dnssrv;
}
```

Of course, you can apply this technique using any classes, and you can combine any CFEngine functions with individual classes to handle special cases. Other useful functions are hostrange() and iprange(), which are specially designed to match ranges of hostnames and IP addresses:

```
bundle agent config
{
  classes:
      # Functional classes
```

```
"websrv"        or => { classmatch("websrv.*"),
                        "testsrv_domain_com" };
"linux_dnssrv" and => { classmatch("dnssrv.*"),
                        "linux" };
# Geographical classes, using IP ranges
"location1"     # 10.1.0.0/16, 10.2.0.0/16, also websrv01-10
  or => { iprange("10.1.0.0/16"), iprange("10.2.0.0/16"),
          hostrange("websrv", "01-10") };
"location2"     # 10.10.0.0/16, also websrv11-20
  or => { iprange("10.10.0.0/16"),
          hostrange("websrv", "11-20") };
}
```

You can combine both hard and soft classes, CFEngine functions and special variables, and any type of class expressions, to express the exact conditions on which you want to act.

Controlling Promise Execution Order

Normallly, CFEngine takes care of properly evaluating variables and classes, by combining normal ordering and multiple evaluation passes (up to three), as described in "Normal Ordering" on page 51. In general terms, when a variable or class changes during a pass, anything that depends on it will be reevaluated on the next pass to account for the change.

There are, however, some special cases in which we may need to force CFEngine's hand a little, and make it evaluate things in a different, specific order. For cases like this, you can tell CFEngine to evaluate certain statements only when some class is defined, and only define that class when the appropriate conditions arise.

A clear example of this technique can be seen in the set_config_values() bundle from the standard library, which we saw described in detail in "Editing /etc/sshd_config" on page 78. I invite you to review the description to see the details of how that particular example works.

In general, when we want to force promise A to evaluate after promise B, when their normal order would be reversed, we should define a class after promise B runs, and condition promise A on that class. A useful function for this type of conditioning is isvariable(), which allows us to check whether a variable has been defined. This contrived example shows the technique in action:

```
bundle agent test
{
  vars:
      "var1" string => "value 1";
    foo::
      "var2" string => "value 2";
  classes:
      "foo" expression => isvariable("var1");
      "bar" expression => isvariable("var2");
```

```
    reports:
      cfengine::
        "var1=$(var1)"
          ifvarclass => "bar";
        "var2=$(var2)";
  }
```

And here is what is happening:

1. In the first pass, $(var1) is defined, but $(var2) isn't because the foo class does not exist. Then, the class foo is defined as true, but bar is false because $(var2) does not exist. In the reports: section, the first message is not printed because bar class is false, so only the "var2" message is printed.

2. In the second pass, $(var2) is defined, because the foo class is now true. Then, in the classes: section, the bar calss is defined as true because variable $(var2) now exists. And finally, in the reports: section, the first message is shown because the bar class is now true. The other message is not printed again because it had been printed already in the previous pass (CFEngine keeps track of which promises it has already fulfilled).

The net result is that the messages from the reports: section are printed in reverse order:

```
$ cf-agent -KI -f ./order-control.cf
R: var2=value 2
R: var1=value 1
```

I would advise you to exercise extreme caution, and to think carefully, before messing with CFEngine's normal ordering. The ordering is there because years of experience have shown that is the order that makes most sense, and CFEngine's variable-and-class convergence mechanisms ensure that, in most cases, the behavior is correct even when things need to be evaluated over multiple passes. If you feel the need to modify the order of execution, it pays to first step back and look at the problem from a different perspective and see if it can be made to function within CFEngine's constraints and rules. Only after this option is completely ruled out should you implement mechanisms like shown above. Document them carefully, because as we saw above, the code can quickly get long and complicated.

## CHAPTER 6

Advanced Topics

Throughout this book we have focused on learning the basic concepts of CFEngine, those that will allow you to set up CFEngine and start using it in a productive manner as soon as possible. However, CFEngine is a vastly more complex framework for configuration management. In this last chapter, I would like to briefly introduce you to some of the more advanced features, so that you can get a taste for the sort of things you can achieve. I will not delve into the full details of the topics presented here, but rather give you some simple examples and pointers to the places where you can find more information.

Setting Up Multiple CFEngine Environments

Like any system that can modify the state of a running machine, CFEngine has the potential to seriously damage your systems if any errors are introduced in its configuration. Due to its very purpose, an error in a CFEngine configuration file can spread almost instantly to a very large number of machines, leaving them incorrectly configured or breaking them completely, rendering them inoperational.

For this reason, it is extremely important to thoroughly test CFEngine configuration files before deploying them to your production machines. One of the best ways to do this is to create different environments for development/testing and production. In this section we will go through some techniques that you can use to achieve this goal.

Ideally, testing environments should be as similar to the production environment as possible, so that the configurations are tested as much as possible in the same way they will be exercised in deployment. My suggestion is to choose a set of your machines for testing. These machines will receive any changes you make to your CFEngine policies as soon as you decide to publish them. Once you are satisfied that the changes behave as intended, they can be made available to the production environment.

Which machines to choose for testing? They should be as close as possible to the production machines and be in regular use. On the other hand, of course, they should be non-critical machines, since they will be subject to possible mistakes in your configuration changes. The world should not end if these machines break. The specific answer depends largely on your environment, but here are some suggesions:

- If you are deploying CFEngine in user workstations, you could include your own machine in the test set. This will allow you to detect fairly soon when something breaks. If you are part of an IT support group, your team members are also good candidates, since they should be able to give you direct feedback and even fix the problem themselves when something breaks. Keep in mind, however, that you should have at least one machine you can use that is not included in the test set, so that if something breaks catastrophically, you will have access to your network and systems to fix things. You could also ask for volunteers among your power users (this depends on the type of users you support—it might be easir to get technically-minded or research-minded users to volunteer), as long as they understand the possible consequences, and are able and willing to give you feedback when things don't go as expected, as well as when they do.

- If you are deploying CFEngine in servers, you could include in your test set, apart from at least one dedicated test machine, some of the less critical servers. This could mean non-critical internal web servers, redundant mirrors of existing servers, and other servers that would not affect critical production work if they go down. Of course, you should be careful to choose servers that are representative of the kinds of servers you are configuring (i.e., web servers, DNS servers, database servers, etc.) so that all your configurations are exercised properly. If you are frequently configuring new servers, you should include some of those new servers in your test set, to fully exercise your policy's initial-configuration abilities.

Once you have defined your environments, you can use CFEngine itself to differentiate betwen them. The technique I am about to show you works well in CFEngine Community, and is also recognized by the CFEngine Nova Mission Portal, so if you choose at some point to upgrade to the commercial version, your environments will be properly handled by the graphical interface.

The trick is to store the files for each environment in a different directory under */var/cfengine/masterfiles/* on the policy hub (which will be copied under */var/cfengine/inputs/* on the clients), and instructing the main *promises.cf* file to load the files from the appropriate directory. The directory structure looks like this:

```
/var/cfengine/masterfiles
  promises.cf
  failsafe.cf
  Possibly other files
  environment_development/
    env_promises.cf
    Possibly other files
  environment_testing/
    env_promises.cf
    Possibly other files
  environment_production/
    env_promises.cf
```

```
          Possibly other files
        environment_none/
           env_promises.cf
          Possibly other files
```

In the main promises.cf file, we need to define which machines belong in each environment, as well as implement a way to tell CFEngine from which directory the files need to be read. We do this through a bundle called environments(), which you need to add to your */var/cfengine/masterfiles/promises.cf* file:

```
bundle common environments
{
  classes:
      "environment_development" or => {  ❶
                                      "hostname1_example_com",
                                      "ipv4_10_1_2_3",
                                     };
      "environment_testing"     or => {
                                      classmatch(".*_test_example_com"),  ❷
                                      "ipv4_10_1_2",
                                      "suse_11",
                                     };
      "environment_production"  or => {
                                      classmatch(".*_example_com"),  ❸
                                      "ipv4_10_1",
                                     };
  vars:
    any::   ❹
      "active" string => "none", policy => "overridable";
    environment_production::
      "active" string => "production", policy => "overridable";
    environment_testing::
      "active" string => "testing", policy => "overridable";
    environment_development::
      "active" string => "development", policy => "overridable";
}
```

In a nutshell, this bundle is first defining three classes called environment_develop ment, environment_testing, and environment_production, and then assigning the name of the environment to the variable $(active). This is how it works:

❶ We define environment_development to be a very specific set of machines. Because the or expression means that environment_development will be true if any of the two classes listed is true, the set will include only the machine called hostname1.exam ple.com and the one with IP address 10.1.2.3 will be included. I'm assuming these would be the machines on which the development takes place, plus those used for immediate testing of new changes made to the policies.

❷ The environment_testing class is defined with a slightly larger set of machines. In this case, we use the classmatch() function to indicate that any machines in the .test.example.com domain will be included. Also, any machines in the 10.1.2.0/24 IP address range will be included.

Remember that CFEngine automatically defines hard classes based on a number of automatically-discovered characteristics of the system in which it is running. Several of those hard classes are based on the current IP addresses of the system. If the current host has IP address 10.1.2.5, CFEngine will automatically define the hard classes ipv4_10_1_2_5, ipv4_10_1_2, ipv4_10_1 and ipv4_10.

The final line of this definition includes all machines with SuSE 11 in the testing environment (those in which the hard class suse_11 is defined). This could be useful, for example, if we are in the process of rolling out SuSE 11—we would like those new machines to be automatically configured using the latest available version of our CFEngine policy. This example also shows you that we can use any CFEngine class (not only those related to hostname or IP address) to define our environments.

❸ Finally, we define class environment_production to include the rest of the network. In this case, we are defining all of .example.com, and the whole 10.1.0.0/16 network, to be the production environment.

❹ Now it is time to store the name of the current environment in a string variable, so that we can use it later on to control which files are read. We assign values to the $(active) variable depending on the class that is defined. Note that we order the classes from most generic (any) to most specific (environment_development). This way, if a host belongs to more than one of these classes (for example, host 10.1.2.5 would have both environment_production and environment_testing defined), the most-specific one (in this case, environment_testing) will be used (the last matching class sets the value of the variable). The $(active) variable is defined using the policy => "overridable" attribute, which makes it possible for its value to be reassigned by later statements.

After the environments() bundle is evaluated, the variable $(environments.active) will contain the name of the environment to which the current machine belongs, or "none" if it didn't match any of the environment classes. We can now use this to load the appropriate *env_promises.cf* file:

```
body common control
{
        inputs => {
                    "cfengine_stdlib.cf",
                    "environment_$(environments.active)/env_promises.cf",   ❶
                  };
        bundlesequence => {
                            "environments",
                            "main",
                            "env_main",   ❷
                          };
        version => "Community Promises.cf 1.0.0";
}
```

❶ We use the $(environments.active) variable as part of the filename to load. So for example, when this variable has the value "production", the file *environment_production/env_promises.cf* will be loaded. You can, of course, load additional files from the environment-specific directory, by making further use of the $(environments.active) variable.

❷ We call the env_main() bundle, which must be defined in all versions of the *env_promises.cf* file, so that evaluation does not fail.

The env_main() bundle can be as simple or as complex as needed. It could be just a jumping off point to multiple other bundles, or a simple report like this:

```
bundle agent env_main
{
  reports:
    cfengine::
      "Environment: $(environments.active)";
}
```

Using a Version-Control System to Separate Environments

One of the most natural mechanisms to separate different types of environments is through the use of version control software. VCS provides many advantages, including the following:

- Keeping track of the changes made to the configuration files. If you need to find the state in which CFEngine was configured months ago, a VCS makes it easy to find the exact state of the configuration files at that point in time.

- Allowing rollback to older versions, in case new versions produce unwanted side effects, or you need to recreate the state of your environment at some point in the past. This is particularly powerful when used with CFEngine—in principle, simply installing an old version of the CFEngine configuration on a system should be enough to roll back the system itself to the state in which it was at that point (at least with respect to the items that are controlled by CFEngine, of course).

- Using tags and branches, you can mark significant points in time, or try out drastic modifications without affecting your main copy of the configuration. This is the particular technique that lends itself to managing different types of environments using a VCS.

The choice of a particular VCS depends on many factors, including your personal preferences and experience, and possibly requirements from your organization. I particularly recommend *Git (http://git-scm.com/)*, because it makes it very easy to develop things in an agile fashion. In conjunction with Git, it is particularly recommended to use a model known as git-flow *(http://nvie.com/posts/a-successful-git-branching -model/)* and an associated tool *(https://github.com/nvie/gitflow)* to make it easier to implement, created by Vincent Driessen. Git-flow specifies a model for keeping track of development and production branches, as well as "feature branches" for making drastic changes to the code without affecting any of the two main branches.

Depending on the size of your environment, you may want to have separate branches for testing and development. This would allow you to continue making changes in the development branch while having a frozen version in the testing environment, for later transfer into production.

 Remember that in this configuration, CFEngine will use files according to the content of the environment-specific directories as documented in "Setting Up Multiple CFEngine Environments" on page 141, regardless of Git branches. Make sure you copy the files from one directory to the other when merging branches, or when deploying them. It is also possible to implement things in such a way that the development and production branches are automatically copied into the environment-specific directories, although that is outside the scope of our current description.

The CFEngine policy hub must be configured to automatically check out the Git repository under the */var/cfengine/masterfiles/* directory, so that the policy files are automatically distributed to all the clients. This is easily done with an entry in */etc/crontab* or could be scheduled through CFEngine. For example, if */var/cfengine/masterfiles/* is already a checked-out version of the Git repository, the following promise can be used to update it every 30 minutes (it should be added to the update() bundle, in */var/cfengine/masterfiles/failsafe.cf* in the commands: section)

```
am_policy_hub&(Min00_05||Min30_35)::
  "/usr/bin/git pull origin"
    contain => u_in_dir("$(master_location)"),
    comment => "Update $(master_location) from git repository",
    handle  => "update_masterfiles_from_git";
...
body contain u_in_dir(s)
{
        chdir => "$(s)";
}
```

Flow of Development and Deployment

The development of new CFEngine policies, or changes to the existing ones, can take place anywhere that the Git repository can be cloned. In my setup, I normally maintain the CFEngine files in my own laptop, making new changes first in the *environment_development* directory and committing them to my local copy of the repository. Once I'm satisfied enough to make them available for testing, I copy them to the *environment_testing* directory and push the repository to the master branch of the Git server.

When new changes are pushed onto the master branch, the policy hub updates */var/cfengine/masterfiles/* from the Git repository, and from there distributes the files to all its clients. Machines in the test group will use the files under *environment_testing*. Thus, when new changes are pushed, they will soon be available automatically for test machines.

At this stage, you should wait and observe the effects of the changes on the test machines.

When you are satisfied with the changes, you can copy the changes to the *environment_production* directory, push the changes to the repository, and wait for them to propagate.

At this point, the new configuration files will be automatically deployed to the production directories of the policy servers, and from there to the production CFEngine clients the next time they request policy updates.

CFEngine Testing

One of the least-explored and perhaps more vaguely-defined topics in configuration management is that of testing. As in any type of development and deployment, testing of changes is essential for ensuring correct operation.

Normally, testing in configuration management systems is done simply by deploying the modified policies in a set of test systems and letting it run, or making some modifications to the system to see if it executes the necessary configuration changes. This is akin to an application developer running his application to try it out and see if there are any unexpected behaviors. While this type of testing is important and necessary, it suffers from the same problems in CM as it does in software development, namely:

- Incompleteness: It is essentially impossible to exercise all possible paths in the code, and in similar ways it is impossible to exercise all possible system states to see if the new policy behaves correctly in all of them.
- Subjectiveness: if the developer tests the software, the testing is necessarily biased by the developer knowing what changes have been made, and (perhaps even unconsciously) testing only behaviors related to that activity. The same problem occurs in CM if the person or team who makes the changes is the same one that tests the changes. This problem can be alleviated by having separate people perform the testing.

What is needed is a more rigorous and disciplined approach to testing configuration management (in this case, CFEngine) policies. I propose you use two types of testing: behavioral testing and unit testing.

Behavioral Testing for CFEngine Policies

In recent years, Behavior-Driven Development (BDD) has emerged as a powerful way of testing software: the expected behavior of the software under different circumstances is described (often in high-level, human-readable language), from which tests are automatically derived. Then the software is developed or modified to pass those tests.

A similar approach can be had with configuration management. The idea is to describe the desired system behavior under different scenarios and inputs, and then develop the configuration-management policies to ensure those behaviors are achieved. This has been described as Behavior-Driven Infrastructure (*http://blogs.oracle.com/martin/entry/behavior_driven_infrastructure*).

Details about these techniques are outside the scope of this book, but I will point you to some resources for further learning:

- Cucumber (*http://cukes.info/*) is a framework for BDD in which desired behaviors are expressed in near-natural language. It was originally developed for Ruby development, but can be extended to perform any kind of testing.
- Cucumber-nagios (*http://auxesis.github.com/cucumber-nagios/*) is a Cucumber extension that operates as a Nagios (*http://www.nagios.org/*) plugin, and thus can be used to verify statements made in Cucumber format using the Nagios functionality.
- Vagrant (*http://vagrantup.com/*) is a system that allows dynamic creation and interaction with virtual machine environments, and thus can be used to automate system creation, configuration, and testing.

Unit Testing for CFEngine Policies

Unit testing refers to testing individual components of a system to ensure they perform their functions appropriately.

As with software development, unit testing can be extremely beneficial to CFEngine policies. A CFEngine policy consists of multiple bundles and body components that perform different configuration functions. As such, these bundles can be individually tested to ensure they perform the desired tasks. Performing unit testing on these components as they are written or modified can provide enormous cost savings when debugging complete policies.

As in software development, I would advise writing unit tests for different components as they are developed, so that the tests can be run when desired, ideally as part of the SCM or build process.

Happily, CFEngine comes with a unit-testing framework included in the distribution, under the *tests/* directory. The *testall* script in this directory is used to run the tests, either individually, by directory or all of them.

An individual test must be a completely self-contained CFEngine policy file (except for libraries or other files that it needs to include as part of the test), and it must contain at least three bundles called init(), test(), and check(). The init() bundle is used to set up the test: to create required input files, for example. The test() bundle is the one that actually performs the test, exercising the functionality that you want to verify.

Finally, the check() bundle verifies whether the test was successful, and reports the result. These three bundles are automatically executed by the *testall* script, and their results collected and presented to the user.

As an example, consider the following CFEngine bundle, which replaces a line in a text file if it matches a regular expression. If the regular expression is not found, the line of text is added to the file. This bundle is part of *cfengine_stdlib.cf*:

```
bundle edit_line replace_or_add(pattern,line)

# Replace a pattern in a file with a single line.
# If the pattern is not found, add the line to the file.
# The pattern must match the whole line (it is automatically
# anchored to the start and end of the line) to avoid
# ambiguity.

{
  vars:
      "cline" string => canonify("$(line)");

  replace_patterns:
      "^(?!$(line)$)$(pattern)$"
        replace_with => value("$(line)"),
        classes => always("replace_done_$(cline)");

  insert_lines:
      "$(line)"
        ifvarclass => "replace_done_$(cline)";
}
```

To build unit tests for this bundle, we must first consider the different cases that we want to test:

1. $(pattern) appears in the text file, so it will be replaced by $(line)
2. $(pattern) does not appear in the text file, so $(line) will be added to the file.

Let's now build a test file for this bundle. All tests are stored inside the *test/* directory of the CFEngine source distribution, and are organized in directories named *xx_category/yy_subcategory/nnn.cf*. In our case, we will store this file as *16_stdlib/01_edit_line/001.cf*.

Since it must be self-contained, it must include a body common control:

```
body common control
{
        inputs => { "../../default.cf.sub",      ❶
                    "../../../../masterfiles/cfengine_stdlib.cf"   ❷
                  };
        bundlesequence  => { default("$(this.promise_filename)") };   ❸
        version => "1.0";
}
```

❶ The testing framework includes a file called *default.cf.sub*, which contains a number of useful utility bundles and bodies for initializing common parameters and variables, for checking test results, etc. We will see a couple of these later, but I encourage you to read it in full to learn everything it contains.

❷ For this particular test, we need to include *cfengine_stdlib.cf*, since the bundle we will test is defined in it. In general, you should not include *cfengine_stdlib.cf* unless it is necessary, to make each test case as stand-alone as possible. Even in this case, you will notice that `replace_or_add()` is the only bundle we use from the standard library. All other bundles and bodies are defined in the test file itself to reduce dependencies and ensure predictability of behavior.

❸ The `bundlesequence` of all tests must call the `default()` bundle, defined in *default.cf.sub*, and which takes care of automatically calling the `init()`, `test()` and `check()` bundles. The variable `$(this.promise_filename)` contains the current filename, and must be passed as argument to `default()` for reporting purposes.

Now we have to define the `init()`, `test()` and `check()` bundles. First comes `init()`:

```
bundle agent init
{
  vars:
      "states" slist => { "actual", "expected" };    ❶

      "actual" string =>    ❷
      "BEGIN
line1 plus more text
END";

      "expected" string =>
      "BEGIN
new line 1
END
new line 2";

  files:
      "$(G.testfile).$(states)"    ❸
        create => "true",
        edit_line => init_insert("$(init.$(states))"),
        edit_defaults => init_empty;
}

bundle edit_line init_insert(str)    ❹
{
  insert_lines:
      "$(str)";
}

body edit_defaults init_empty
{
      empty_file_before_editing => "true";
}
```

❶ We define a list called @(states) with the names of the two variables we will define next. This will help in simplifying the policy by using list expansion to create the test files.

❷ We define two variables called $(actual) and $(expected). The text in $(actual) will be used as the starting point for the test, and the test operations will be applied to it. The text in $(expected) is the expected end result of the test, and will be compared to the final result to check whether the test passed or failed.

❸ Finally, we use a files: promise to write the values of $(actual) and $(expected) to two files, using the values in @(states) to loop over the variables. The variable $(G.testfile) is defined in *default.cf.sub* as a default base filename for use with the tests, along with some other variables:

```
temp_declared::
  "testroot" string => getenv("TEMP", "65535");
  "testdir"  string => concat(getenv("TEMP", "65535"), "/TEST.cfengine");
  "testfile" string => concat(getenv("TEMP", "65535"), "/TEST.cfengine");
!temp_declared::
  "testroot" string => "/tmp";
  "testdir"  string => "/tmp/TEST.cfengine";
  "testfile" string => "/tmp/TEST.cfengine";
```

As you can see, the default value of $(G.testfile) is "/tmp/TEST.cfengine", unless the TEMP environment variable is defined, in which case the value of TEMP is used instead of "/tmp/" to construct the filename. The value of $(G.testfile) is concatenated with the different values in @(states), so that the two files created in this example will be */tmp/TEST.cfengine.actual* and */tmp/TEST.cfengine.expected*, containing the values of $(actual) and $(expected), respectively.

❹ The init_insert() bundle and the init_empty body are used by the files: promise that creates the files, and are declared here as well. Both of these components have equivalents in the standard library, but as we said before, we avoid using them to reduce external dependencies to a minimum.

After init() runs, the test inputs are ready: the edit operations will be applied on */tmp/TEST.cfengine.actual*, and at the end its contents will be compared to */tmp/TEST.cfengine.expected* to determine if the test was successful. We are now ready to run the actual test:

```
bundle agent test
{
  vars:
      "tpat1" string => "line1.*";       ❶
      "tstr1" string => "new line 1";
      "tpat2" string => "line2.*";
      "tstr2" string => "new line 2";

  files:
      "$(G.testfile).actual"       ❷
        create => "false",
        edit_line => replace_or_add("$(test.tpat1)", "$(test.tstr1)");
```

```
            "$(G.testfile).actual"
              create => "false",
              edit_line => replace_or_add("$(test.tpat2)", "$(test.tstr2)");
      }
```

❶ We first define some variables for use in the test. In this case, we are going to perform two calls to `replace_or_add()`, as dictated by the two cases we want to test. For this, we define two pairs of variables containing the pattern and line for each of the two cases.

❷ Finally! We get to the meat of the test. In the `files:` section, we have two promises on the "actual" file. The first one replaces a line that already exists (`"line1.*"`) with some new text. The second one is called with a pattern that does not appear in the original file (`"line2.*"`), so a new line should be added to the file.

That's it. In most cases, the setup is the most complicated part of a test; the actual execution of the test is quite simple. After `test()` is done, we will have in */tmp/ TEST.cfengine.actual* the result of the operations on the original file, and in */tmp/ TEST.cfengine.expected* the expected result. It is time to verify the results of the test:

```
bundle agent check
{
  methods:
      "any" usebundle => default_check_diff("$(G.testfile).actual",
                                             "$(G.testfile).expected",
                                             "$(this.promise_filename)");
}
```

In this bundle, we simply have a call to the `default_check_diff()` bundle, which is also defined in *default.cf.sub*. It receives as arguments the two files to compare and the test filename. If the files are the same, it simply produces a "pass" result. If the files differ, it produces a "fail" result, plus copious log output (*diff* result, plus full content and hex dump of both files) to allow you to debug the problem.

When writing your own tests, remember that the output from the tests must contain "*<testname>* Pass" if the test passes, and "*<testname>* FAIL" if the test fails. Anything else (in fact, all output, including the Pass/Fail string) is written to the *test.log* file so you can determine exactly what happened.

Well, let's now run the test! By default *testall* executes all the tests (which you should try sometime), but for now we will just run the new test we wrote:

```
$ cd cfengine-3.3.0/tests
$ ./testall 16_stdlib/01_edit_line/001.cf
========================================================================
Testsuite started at 2012-01-26 22:52:57
------------------------------------------------------------------------
Total tests: 1

-n ./16_stdlib/01_edit_line/001.cf
Pass

========================================================================
```

```
Testsuite finished at 2012-01-26 22:52:57 (0 seconds)

Passed tests: 1
Failed tests: 0
Failed to crash tests: 0
Skipped tests: 0
```

Now, let's imagine we made a mistake in the replace_or_add() bundle, and inverted the logic on the test for the insert_lines: promise (note the added ! sign):

```
insert_lines:
  "$(line)"
    ifvarclass => "!replace_done_$(cline)";
```

This will produce the wrong output, and it will be caught by the test:

```
$ ./testall 16_stdlib/01_edit_line/001.cf
======================================================================
Testsuite started at 2012-01-26 23:03:34
----------------------------------------------------------------------
Total tests: 1

-n ./16_stdlib/01_edit_line/001.cf
FAIL (UNEXPECTED FAILURE)


======================================================================
Testsuite finished at 2012-01-26 23:03:34 (0 seconds)

Passed tests: 0
Failed tests: 1
Failed to crash tests: 0
Skipped tests: 0
```

We can now look at *test.log* to see the details of the failure. Among a lot of other information, we can find the output of the diff command between the expected and actual files:

```
R: --- /Users/a10022/CFEngine/src/core/tests/acceptance/workdir/...
+++ /Users/a10022/CFEngine/src/core/tests/acceptance/workdir/...
@@ -1,4 +1,5 @@
 BEGIN
 new line 1
 END
+new line 1
 new line 2
```

This will give you already a hint of what the problem was. The line is being inserted even though it exists already in the file.

Of course, the tests can be arbitrarily complex, since they are full CFEngine bundles. In our case both test cases of the bundle are being tested together—if one of them fails, the whole test fails. Alternatively, we could have the script test the two possible cases separately: first on a file where a line is to be replaced, then on a file where a new line is to be added. This would make it easier to distinguish which part of the bundle is failing. The level of granularity used for the unit tests needs to be decided on a case by case basis depending on the bundle that is being tested and the complexity of its inputs.

In this example I have shown you a very simple example, easy to replicate and test on its own. What do you do for CFEngine bundles that effect more profound changes in a system, and whose input cannot be easily replicated? For example, how do you unit-test a bundle that manages system users? There is no single answer to this. For example, for manipulation of system files, you could set up copies of the real files under /tmp, and run the tests on them. For other system components, you may need to create custom programs to emulate their behavior. For testing package management, the test suite already includes the *mock-package-manager* program, which you can set to an arbitrary state (installed packages, for example) during the init() bundle, and query or modify during the test() bundle, without having to actually install or modify anything on the system.

A large number of tests are distributed with CFEngine. I encourage you to look at them to learn the capabilities of the framework, and to use it for testing all your bundles.

Where to from Here?

In the course of this book we have discussed many concepts and techniques for effectively using CFEngine to manage computer systems. Whether you are managing your own machine, a network of five machines, or a Google-sized datacenter, the same basic principles apply. Still, we have only scratched the surface, even with the more advanced topics we explored in this last chapter. CFEngine is a rich and complex tool, and it has capabilities way beyond what we have covered here. I expect to have given you a running start, but it is up to you to continue experimenting, discovering and evolving. I encourage you to read CFEngine's abundant documentation to learn many of the more advanced capabilities. I also encourage you to take advantage of the friendly and helpful CFEngine community, in which both users and developers participate to provide a helping hand and to discuss the future of CFEngine.

There are many aspects of CFEngine functionality that we have not touched in this book, including the capabilities of the knowledge management tools included in CFEngine, database integration, and advanced Windows configuration facilities. Many of these advanced capabilities are limited to (or better developed in) the commercial editions of CFEngine. Many others, however, are available in the Community edition. Practice makes perfect, and there is no single way of achieving many tasks in CFEngine. As you learn more, you will develop better and more efficient ways of achieving the same tasks. As you become familiar with the syntax and the constructs available in the language, you will discover more advanced ways of using the tool.

A word of caution: CFEngine is not suited for every single system-management application. While it is great for many configuration tasks, it may lack the power provided by specialized tools for some particular areas. For example, you can use CFEngine to configure a backup utility, but the utility itself is probably much more suited for actually scheduling and performing the backups. Other tasks for which specialized tools may be better suited include network monitoring, intrusion detection, inventory, and user management. The mark of a good sysadmin is the use of the right tools for the right task. CFEngine is now one more tool in your arsenal, a very flexible tool, and as such is able to integrate properly in many different situations and environments. Hopefully, after reading this book, you will be able to see ways in which CFEngine can integrate into your existing environment and make it better, possibly aiding also the configuration and management of some of the specialized tools that you use.

CFEngine is constantly evolving. You can watch this evolution in action, and even contribute to it, by participating in the CFEngine community. Whether you post in the forums, write in your blog, teach CFEngine to your coworkers, or simply spread the word about it, you will be participating in the development of one of the oldest and longest-living configuration management tools in existence. With CFEngine 3, the foundations are laid for a much smoother evolution path, grounded in strong computer science theory and with the mechanisms in place to develop new features with much less friction than in the past. In this situation, the CFEngine developers are now, more than ever before, open to comments, questions and suggestions by users that help them better understand the needs, and if new worthwhile features are suggested, or better ways of achieving certain tasks are proposed, there is a good chance that they will be implemented.

More than anything else, I encourage you to experiment and have fun. There are few things as satisfying to a system administrator as having systems running smoothly and with as little human intervention as possible. Play with CFEngine to explore its capabilities, try new things, break things (in a controlled manner whenever possible! We don't want you to get fired) and learn new tricks. The basic principle of CFEngine is *convergent configuration*, and over time your systems will converge to a stable situation. As your CFEngine policies evolve and stabilize, you will be able to free your mind from mundane day-to-day details. And this is the whole purpose of CFEngine: to elevate your thinking about your systems—to enable you to manage them through expressions of intent. CFEngine will implement the details and give you knowledge that you can use to further improve your infrastructure. CFEngine allows you to become much more than a sysadmin—it makes you an *infrastructure engineer*.

Enjoy the ride.

Editing CFEngine 3 Configurations in Emacs

Ted Zlatanov

If you are an Emacs user, you will not be surprised to learn that there is an Emacs mode for editing CFEngine configuration files. In this Appendix you will learn how to set up and use the CFEngine editing mode in Emacs.

Setting Up

You need GNU Emacs 23.1 or higher. Earlier versions or XEmacs may work as well, but have not been extensively tested.

First, you need to download *cfengine.el* from *https://raw.github.com/cfengine/core/master/contrib/cfengine.el*. Emacs currently includes an older version of this file. Emacs 24.2 and higher, when released, will include the latest version, but 24.1 and earlier do not, so you need to manually download it.

Assuming you have downloaded the library to your computer, you can add it to your load path. Follow the generic instructions from the Emacs wiki (*http://www.emacswiki.org/emacs/LoadPath#toc1*), or just put the following code in your *.emacs* file:

```
(autoload 'cfengine-mode "cfengine" "cfengine editing" t)
(add-to-list 'load-path "/directory/where/the/library/lives/")
```

You will probably want to tell Emacs to associate *.cf* files with the cfengine-mode, although that could cause problems if you use other files ending with *.cf*. See *http://www.emacswiki.org/emacs/AutoModeAlist* for more information or just add the following line to your *.emacs* file:

```
(add-to-list 'auto-mode-alist '("\\.cf\\'" . cfengine-mode))
```

If you use other files ending with *.cf* and would prefer not to associate this extension with cfengine-mode by default, just run M-x cfengine-mode after you open the file and it will switch to the CFEngine mode.

Using the cfengine Mode

The Emacs Lisp function cfengine-mode is actually a wrapper that tries to figure out if you are editing CFEngine 3 or CFEngine 2 configurations. If you open a blank file, it will assume CFEngine 2, but the next time it has some text to examine, it will do the right thing. To eliminate the uncertainty, replace cfengine-mode with cfengine3-mode in the previous section. It does the exact same thing except it always assumes CFEngine 3 syntax.

After you open a file with cfengine-mode, in the Emacs modeline (the summary status bar under the content) you will see CFE2 or CFE3. That tells you unambiguously which one is the active mode.

You can now edit the file. Hurrah! Type your masterpiece. The CFEngine mode offers some very useful commands. The following list summarize those I use a lot, but the Emacs command set contains a lot more that can apply. Each command is shown with both its default keybinding and the name of the function that invokes it.

 M-h means hitting either the Alt or Meta key, depending on your keyboard, together with "h," or hitting the ESC key followed by the "h" key. C-M-h means the same thing, but holding down the Ctrl key as well.

M-h (mark-paragraph)
 Select a "paragraph" of text (delimited by empty lines).
C-M-h (mark-defun)
 Select the whole bundle or body surrounding the cursor.
C-M-a (beginning-defun)
 Move to the beginning of the current bundle or body, or to the previous one if the cursor is already at the beginning of it.
C-M-e (end-of-defun)
 Move to the end of the current bundle or body, or the next one if the cursor is already at the end of it.
TAB (indent-for-tab-command)
 Indent the current line. The exact indentation depends on how you have set your cfengine-parameters-indent variable, which is explained in the next section.

Once you are in `cfengine-mode`, syntax highlighting will be done according to CFEngine syntax, and indentation will be done according to the parameters described in the following section.

There are many other editing commands available in `cfengine-mode` that are inherited from the Emacs general text editing facilities. Explore Emacs and you will be able to edit not just CFEngine configurations, but other kinds of text and code easily and efficiently.

General information about Emacs can be found in its copious Info files, and in *Learning GNU Emacs*, by Debra Cameron, James Elliott, Marc Loy, Eric S. Raymond, and Bill Rosenblatt (O'Reilly).

Customizing Indentation in cfengine-mode

You need to customize only two parameters to control indentation in `cfengine-mode`. Do this by typing M-x `customize-variable` and then typing the parameter name (you can use TAB completion so you don't have to type it out).

> After you change any variable, make sure you save your changes in your *~/.emacs* or in comments in your CFEngine configuration file, or the changes will take effect only until the end of your current Emacs session.

`cfengine-indent`
> The size in spaces of one "indentation step." Default value is 2.
>
> The indentation step is the basic unit of measure for indenting different parts of a CFEngine policy:
> - The start of a `bundle` or `body` declaration is indented zero steps (starts at the first column).
> - A promise type section (e.g. `vars:` or `files:`) is indented one step.
> - A class selector line (e.g. `cfengine::`) is indented two steps.
> - A promise is indented three steps. Indentation within the promise is done according to the settings of `cfengine-parameters-indent`, described later.
> - Attributes inside `body` declarations are indented as if they were promise attributes, according to the rules set by `cfengine-parameters-indent`.
>
> Note that these indentation steps remain even when one of the elements before is not present. This means that a promise will always be indented three steps, even when it is not preceded by a class selector line. The idea is that all the elements of the same type are indented consistently throughout the policy file.

cfengine-parameters-indent
> Indentation of CFEngine 3 promise parameters and of attributes in compound body declarations.

This is the screen you will see when you choose to customize this variable:

```
Cfengine Parameters Indent:
Choice: [Value Menu] Anchor at beginning of promise
Choice: [Value Menu] Indent parameter name
Indentation amount from anchor: 0
```

To understand what the different parts of the parameter mean, consider this code as reference:

```
bundle x y
{
  section:
    class::
       "promiser"
       promiseparameter => value;
}
```

In the first choice, you select whether `promiseparameter` will be anchored "at the beginning of the line" (absolutely) or "at the beginning of the promise" (relative to `"promiser"`). In the second choice, you select whether you want to "indent the parameter name" (the start of the word `promiseparameter` will be indented to a certain position) or to "indent the arrow" (this means that the position of the arrow that separates the parameter and its value will be calculated, and the rest of the line will be oriented around it). Finally, you can choose the amount of the indentation, in spaces.

The default is to anchor at promise, indent parameter name, and offset by 0 characters, which results in this (observe that, according to these parameters, the promise attributes, `comment` and `perms`, start at the same column as the promiser `"/tmp/netrc"`):

```
bundle agent rcfiles
{
  files:
    any::
       "/tmp/netrc"
       comment => "my netrc",
       perms => mog("600", "tzz", "tzz");
}
```

If we change the offset to 2, we get this (promise attributes are indented two spaces with respect to the promiser):

```
bundle agent rcfiles
{
  files:
    any::
       "/tmp/netrc"
         comment => "my netrc",
         perms => mog("600", "tzz", "tzz");
}
```

If we choose "anchor at the beginning of line," "indent the arrow," and offset by 10, we get this (the arrows in the parameters start at column 10 counted from the beginning of the line):

```
bundle agent rcfiles
{
  files:
    any::
      "/tmp/netrc"
    comment => "my netrc",
      perms => mog("600", "tzz", "tzz");
}
```

Some coders, including the author of *cfengine_stdlib.cf*, like to "anchor at promise," "indent arrow," and offset 16 (in this case, the arrows start 16 columns after the promiser):

```
bundle agent rcfiles
{
  files:
    any::
      "/tmp/netrc"
              comment => "my netrc",
                perms => mog("600", "tzz", "tzz");
}
```

About the Author

Diego Zamboni is a computer scientist, consultant, programmer, sysadmin, and overall geek who works as Senior Security Advisor at CFEngine AS. He has more than 20 years of experience in system administration and security, and has worked in both the applied and theoretical sides of the computer science field. He holds a Ph.D. from Purdue University, has worked as a sysadmin at a supercomputer center, as a researcher at the IBM Zurich Research Lab, and as a consultant at HP Enterprise Services. These days, he splits his time between coming up with new security-related projects at CFEngine, nurturing the CFEngine community, coding useful CFEngine policies, and spending time with his family. He lives in Queretaro, Mexico with his wife and two daughters.

Have it your way.

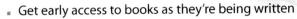

Get even more for your money.

Join the O'Reilly Community, and register the O'Reilly books you own. It's free, and you'll get:

- $4.99 ebook upgrade offer
- 40% upgrade offer on O'Reilly print books
- Membership discounts on books and events
- Free lifetime updates to ebooks and videos
- Multiple ebook formats, DRM FREE
- Participation in the O'Reilly community
- Newsletters
- Account management
- 100% Satisfaction Guarantee

Signing up is easy:

1. Go to: oreilly.com/go/register
2. Create an O'Reilly login.
3. Provide your address.
4. Register your books.

Note: English-language books only

To order books online:
oreilly.com/store

For questions about products or an order:
orders@oreilly.com

To sign up to get topic-specific email announcements and/or news about upcoming books, conferences, special offers, and new technologies:
elists@oreilly.com

For technical questions about book content:
booktech@oreilly.com

To submit new book proposals to our editors:
proposals@oreilly.com

O'Reilly books are available in multiple DRM-free ebook formats. For more information:
oreilly.com/ebooks

O'REILLY®

Spreading the knowledge of innovators   oreilly.com

CPSIA information can be obtained at www.ICGtesting.com
Printed in the USA
LVOW051928120412

277382LV00001B/1/P